Compassion Without Compromise

Leaving a Legacy of Faith

Jennifer Stengel-Mohr

&

William J. Mohr

The primary Bible version referenced in this book is the New International Version. Scriptures from other versions are noted next to the scripture.

ISBN: 978-1-957294-10-0

R.D. Talley Books Publishing, LLC
4882 W. Lone Mountain Road
Las Vegas, Nevada 89130
www.rdtalleybooks.com

Dedication

To all those people in the generations before us who cared enough to give us Jesus. For those who loved us, guided us and set our feet on the path to righteousness. We are grateful for all the prayers of the faithful that have allowed us to stay the course. We pray that we are able to do the same for those who come after us.

Author's Note

In order to better understand the context of this book, you will need to understand the differences between the following:

*The Church- the body of Christ, a group of true believers

*church(es)- any church in general, the physical place

Our goal is not to persuade anyone into or away from a particular denomination. We also do not intend to minimize the importance of attending church or being part of a local body of believers.

Joshua Reads the Book of the Law to the People

30 Joshua built an altar to honor the LORD, the God of Israel. He built it on Mount Ebal. **31** Moses, the servant of the LORD, had commanded the Israelites to do that. Joshua built the altar according to what is written in the Book of the Law of Moses. Joshua built the altar out of stones that iron tools had never touched. Then the people offered on the altar burnt offerings to the LORD. They also sacrificed friendship offerings on it. **32** Joshua copied the law of Moses on stones. He did it while all the Israelites were watching. **33** They were standing on both sides of the ark of the covenant of the LORD. All the Israelites, including outsiders and citizens, were there. Israel's elders, officials and judges were also there. All of them faced the priests, who were Levites. They were carrying the ark. Half of the people stood in front of Mount Gerizim. The other half stood in front of Mount Ebal. Moses, the servant of the LORD, had earlier told them to do it. Moses told them to do it when he had given directions to bless the Israelites.

34 Then Joshua read all the words of the law out loud. He read the blessings and the curses. He read them just as they are written in the Book of the Law. **35** Joshua read every word Moses had commanded. He read them to the whole community of Israel.

That included the women and children. It also included the outsiders living among them.

Joshua 8:30-35

Let us boldly follow the example of Joshua and bring about in our generation honor, reverence and sacrifice for the Lord and knowledge of His Word to all people!

Preface

Now to him who is able to do immeasurably more than all we ask or imagine, according to his power that is at work within us, ²¹ to him be glory in the church and in Christ Jesus throughout all generations, for ever and ever! Amen.

Ephesians 3:20-21

After having authored two faith-based books, I believed strongly that in order to really understand the next generation, I needed to add a younger person's perspective. I wanted to gain insights from someone who was walking the walk of faith based on today's realities. Although God and His Word does not change, society definitely does.

In order to reach this generation, as well as future generations, it is imperative that we understand them intimately by knowing the challenges they face and the beliefs that they hold. To that end, my son has been a substantial contributor to this book. It was important to have his perspective so it would be effective in accomplishing its goals in reaching the next generation.

My son is strong in faith in his own right and has become a sounding board and debate partner for me for several years. Having been homeschooled and raised in the church, he thinks differently than most in his generation. However, I have realized that like many of his peers who were raised in a similar way, God has given him favor in these times and has put him in places of influence.

I can recall an impression in my spirit as I read Daniel 1:17-21. In these verses it tells us that Daniel and his friends found favor with the King because their knowledge, wisdom and skills were unmatched by any in the land. This was significant since Daniel and his friends were not of "the system". I immediately made the association with those of this generation who were raised like my son. They grew up with a different perspective than most of society but are now able to intercede in society in positive and valuable ways as a result of being able to think differently.

God's favor was upon Daniel and his friends because they did not submit to the authority of the King when it contradicted the authority of God. I have hope for the future, first because my hope is in Christ, not in this world. But also because God always promises a remnant. I believe there is a strong core of faith-filled youth that have been raised to carry-on the faith to the next generation. However, we need to continue to nurture, guide and provide support for their battle ahead.

This book offers insights on how to work within the challenges of today's society and use them as opportunities to advance the Kingdom. God's Word confirms multiple times that he cares about generations. Our sincere hope is that this book will encourage and inspire you to be bold in faith and have a positive impact on those around you for generations to come.

Table of Contents

Introduction

Your kingdom is an everlasting kingdom, And Your dominion endures throughout all generations.

Psalm 145:13

God is the god of eternity. Unlike humans who mostly think in the here and now, God thinks about generations. He has a plan and sees the beginning from the end. We play a critical role in this plan. If it were not so, He would not have sent His most precious gift, Jesus, His only son, to save us and to bridge this gap which gives us direct access to Him.

While God has ultimate authority, He has seen fit to give us a specific role to play in the advancement of His Kingdom. He has called us to be The Church and He has empowered us with the Holy Spirit to be His hands and feet on this earth, which will result in eternal impact. This is not something to be taken lightly and this is not just something we do in our spare time, but this is our purpose. Regardless of what titles we have or positions we hold, advancing the Kingdom should be our goal.

Each of us has a sphere of influence. This can be our home, our friends, our job, our community or our church. We have an integral role to play in spreading the message of Christ and being the daily reminder of His Word to others. You might be the only Bible someone reads. D.L. Moodly, a well-known theologian once said, "Out of 100 people, 1 will read the Bible, the other 99 will read the Christian." Each person we meet is an opportunity to point them to Christ, not just with our words, but more importantly, with our actions. When we do this, it doesn't just affect our lives, but it influences those around us. So, are we fulfilling this role?

God's timing is always perfect. After 400 years of silence, God chose a very specific time and place to send Jesus into the world. The Romans ruled over much of the world and they made many advancements in society.

They had developed innovative medical treatments, engineered marvels such as the aqueducts and refined the roadway systems for better travel, which also led to increased communication. However, it was also a time of great moral decay. A desire for riches, a lifestyle of lasciviousness and a lack of respect for human life was common. Mass murders, gladiators taking lives thoughtlessly and deadly violence was looked upon as sport and spectacle.

Aside from Judaism (the traditional Jewish belief in one God), Paganism was the widely-held religious view of the time. Paganism is the belief that nature and the things of it, including humans, have spiritual significance, yet there was no single divine power. Paganism often includes the worship of many gods who oversee various elements of nature. The pagan worldview was driving decision-making in all realms of life.

Simultaneously during this time, there was a great interest in gaining wisdom and knowledge; however, the sources of this knowledge were diverse and ever changing. There was a weaving of many cultural and spiritual beliefs into a collective mindset that was self-destructive and harmful to society as a whole. Ultimately, these factors lead to the collapse of the Roman Empire. In many ways, the world that we are living in today is much like the way things were when Jesus came to earth.

Jesus is the only hope! Our children and our children's children need to embrace this understanding. However, how many of those in today's generation actually know who Christ really is? We can blame this on so many things, but we have to recognize our responsibility in this and in the generation before us so we can move to action to bring about change. The time is now!

For thousands of years the Israelites had been waiting for the promised Messiah, yet when Jesus did arrive, some did not recognize Him and others denied who He was. This was not for lack of knowledge, because they had all of the writings of the prophets, which were extremely specific about who the Messiah would be. But it was because their worldly perspective did not match who they thought Jesus was.

Again, this is very similar to today's situation. Many will not embrace Jesus because they truly do not know who He is or what the Bible actually says about Him. There are so many counterfeit versions of Christ. Society wants to embrace a Jesus that is all love without repentance. They want a Jesus of their own making. These versions represent a huge compromise of who Jesus really is! This error in judgment is due in part to a lack of biblical literacy. Many Christians truly do not know what scripture actually says about any number of vital topics, particularly God's Will and who Jesus is.

Jesus did not come as the warrior that most people expected, as the one would who save them from political oppression. Jesus did not come to bring unity, he came to divide those who are God's and those who are of the world. Luke 12:49-53 describes this in detail:

49 "I have come to bring fire on the earth, and how I wish it were already kindled! 50 But I have a baptism to undergo, and what constraint I am under until it is completed! 51 Do you think I came to bring peace on earth? No, I tell you, but division. 52 From now on there will be five in one family divided against each other, three against two and two against three. 53 They will be divided, father against son and son against father, mother against daughter and daughter against mother, mother-in-law against daughter-in-law and daughter-in-law against mother-in-law." This tells us to be on guard in our own families as there will be those who will not accept Christ.

Jesus came with a wisdom that had not been perceived before. He came with a language that had not been heard before. He came with a mission that had not been witnessed before. Jesus was so strikingly different from what was commonplace at the time, which caused many to be confounded, yet it also caused people to take notice.

Jesus encountered everyone and every situation with compassion. He had a heart for those who were hurting. Compassion is what moved Him to heal, to minister and ultimately to give His life. But we cannot overlook the fact that He also was relentless in standing for the truth of God's Word. He was the Truth! So, in this respect, He never compromised. He only did what he saw and heard The Father do.

In God's divine timing, He picked that place and time because the world needed Jesus. And maybe never before since, have we needed Him so badly again. We know the promise of scripture tells us that Jesus will return again, although we do not know when. So, what should we do until then? We are told to occupy until he comes (Luke 19:13). But for many so-called Christians, they have left their posts. Not only is the Christian worldview not being passed on to our children, but in many cases, it is no longer even being practiced by the believer.

We are called to live like He did, love like He did and respond like He did! So our job is to model ourselves after Jesus in how we handle ourselves in a world that does not know Him. This is not easy when there has become a societal and generational divide. We have come to a place where people are co-existing with completely different foundational perspectives, so much so that logic and reason cannot bridge the gap. How do we have tough conversations across generations? How do we introduce scripture to those who don't believe? How do we hold on to what was given to us?

Make no mistake; God's Will shall prevail! The question is, will we be part of it? Those who are following The Spirit are on the move and they are doing what they are called to do. However, the lukewarm Christians are dangerously riding the line and finding themselves lost to the mindset of this world at an alarming rate. We need to have courage and take a stand for faith, even if that means we will fall out of favor with the world.

There are two main principles that guide the structure of this book. The first is the fact that we need to think beyond ourselves and consider future generations. Our goal should be to leave a legacy of faith. This is primarily addressed in the first two chapters, as we discuss what generational faith is and why this is so important.

One of the key mechanisms for moving forward generationally can be found in the advice given to the end-time churches of Revelation. These insights form the foundation for how we can have lasting impact in the faith. The introduction to this principle is addressed in chapter 3. However, each of the remaining chapters of this book dig deeply into one of the insights provided to the specific churches. Applying the advice given to these churches is the way in which we can secure faith for generations to come.

It is our prayer that this book will be a catalyst for moving you with compassion for those around you. We pray that the Holy Spirit gives you the courage you need to be uncompromising in your daily interactions. God bless you on this journey.

In Pursuit

But seek first his kingdom and his righteousness,
and all these things will be given to you as well.

Matthew 6:33

Before we can have an impact or influence on anyone else, we need to know where we stand and what we believe. What are we seeking after in life? The answers to these questions will determine every choice we make in our lives. According to Matthew 6:33, God tells us the answer to this. It should be His Kingdom, and when we do, then everything else falls in line behind that.

We are at a critical juncture in the faith, as the world has slowly been introducing a new 'Jesus' and a new 'gospel' that parallels the desires of the world. This has drawn many people to consider turning to Jesus, due to the fact that this new 'Jesus' fits into their life. This is not the Jesus of scripture who tells us to leave all behind and follow Him.

As this newfound 'Jesus' has gained popularity, some aspects of this mindset have seeped into the Church. The level of deception amongst believers is staggering. The concern has become, 'what do those who profess to be Christians actually believe and know about Jesus?'

We are told that we can know the authenticity of a believer by their fruit. Therefore, we need to examine the lifestyle being led by the 'Christians' around us. In terms of this, it's quite sad and disheartening to see some of the things that 'believers' associate themselves with and promote. This is true for high-profile Christians as well as everyday folks. In all sincerity, this is not in a judgmental manner, but rather a discerning manner that I make these observations. There is a strong disconnect between a profession of faith and a righteous walk in that faith.

The second key in Matthew 6:33 is that we should be seeking His righteousness. While there is absolutely no expectation of perfection in anyone's behavior, as it is not possible, there are however certain non-negotiable choices that one must consider if they are truly a follower of Christ. What I am referring to here are moral and character choices, not things such as negative behaviors or addictions, and the like. These are choices that have significant moral weight and absolutely go against biblical principles that are foundational to the faith. These are things that at some level should even go against one's own spiritual awareness as believers.

For several years now in my spirit, I keep recalling Matthew 7:14, *"narrow is the way"*. When I was writing one of my previous books, God highlighted this verse for me so clearly and confirmed in my spirit, that as humans we truly do not understand just how narrow that way is. In essence, this is the challenge of all humanity. How do we live in the flesh, but not walk in it? Too many 'Christians' today falsely believe they can have one foot in the world and one foot in the Kingdom and ride the line. I believe this is due in part to many 'Christian' influencers who have allowed believers to feel comfortable in their lifestyle while it clearly goes against the Word of God.

The idea that God is all love and no repentance is so dangerous. Some of the scariest verses in scripture are Matthew 7: 21-23, where Jesus basically says that even though some profess to walk and work according to His name, He says He does not know them.

I am not very fond of the phrase 'falling down a rabbit hole', so I will say that this content is inspired by more of an unraveling. God placed one idea in my spirit, and then the next and so on and so forth. By the time I had gotten to writing this down, it was a fully realized revelation with deep implications beyond just my own spiritual development and edification. I decided to put this in print to share so others could gain perspective and benefit from what God has walked me through. Although this is personally based and testimonial in nature, I feel as if there is divine inspiration behind it and it is grounded in scriptural foundations so others can benefit from it.

In 2023, God gave me the word *simplify* as my word for the following year. Being a type-A personality, a planner and someone who finds it difficult to say 'no', this was a huge undertaking for me. I asked God to guide me on how to simplify. My spirit confirmed that an easy way to simplify was to hold everything to one simple question- **Does it glorify God?** If the answer was no, then it must be removed. Imagine if this were to be applied in every aspect of our life. Simplification could truly be possible and rather straightforward in this respect. However, it doesn't mean that it would be easy.

The guiding verse to go along with this newfound perspective was 1 Timothy 6:6, *"godliness with contentment is great gain."* What exactly does that mean? Essentially, this means living a life according to God's Word and Will and being satisfied and fulfilled by that alone. Easier said than done, right? I can visualize from scripture the heavenly hosts of angels whose job is solely to gather around to worship and praise God with chants and singing for all of eternity. Unfortunately, as humans we have a fleshly body that is accountable to earthly responsibilities as well. So how do we worship God properly while on earth?

How do we learn to be content with what God offers and not seek to chase after what the rest of the world tells us makes us happy?

I found further guidance and support again from Matthew 6:33. *Therefore, seek first...,* this does not mean that we cannot enjoy the things we encounter in this life which are blessings from God, but rather that our pursuit is not after these things, it is after God alone! Then everything else has purpose and meaning because they are in their rightful place below God and in alignment with His Word and Will.

When God is our focus, things align in such a way that is clear, focused, simple and meaningful. Since I was on a journey to apply simplification to all aspects of my life, this included my ministry. I started a women's ministry in 2010 by the leading of the Holy Spirit, and it has grown exponentially each year since. As I was writing this, I found myself at a critical juncture in terms of its future direction. Was I to forge ahead and seek growth, which could potentially double the size of the ministry within a year, or apply this perspective of simplification and move forward prudently so as to not lose sight of the ministry's original purpose? I decided on the latter and had great peace in my spirit about this decision.

This new revelation was one of the key perspectives that led me to more deeply examine my ministry and The Church in general. However, my interest in The Church began long ago as I witnessed so many of my family, friends and acquaintances share their testimonies of faith, growing up in church or leaving their church. From the insights gained from these testimonies, I felt a heavy burden, especially for those hurt by the church in some way. It grieved me that someone would step away from God due to pain or misleading from another person of the faith. God is so good and others should feel the same way about Him. It led me to ponder how we could build back God's reputation that had been tarnished by other 'believers'? Some of this hurt and brokenness was deep.

When I started the ministry, it was made clear to me in the spirit that it needed to develop and function separately from a church affiliation. I was not completely sure why at the time, but I was obedient to that and still hold to it today. Only now do I know why. This ministry was to become a beacon for those who did not have a home church or had been transitioning from their church but needed connection and encouragement in faith. It was an open door for those who had been hurt or questioning their faith to walk in and start to rebuild. Paul tells us in 1 Thessalonians 5:11 as we prepare for the Day of the Lord's return that we need to *continually encourage one another and build each other up*. Positive interactions with other believers started to pave the way for recovery. We have seen so many participants in the ministry recommit to Christ, and even accept Him for the first time. Building relationships was essential in this.

So, why are there so many seeking spiritual encouragement outside the church? It became evident that it was because for many, the church was not providing it. In a number of cases, church has been seen as tradition or obligation, not a place where one can truly connect with God or their faith. One thing that I found quite shocking was when I asked those who were in need of encouragement in their faith, what they believed or why they believed it, there was not a clear sense of that at all. Often, it was a stammering response that was superficial and rarely had any scriptural foundation. These 'believers' did not even know what they believed. Yet for many, they faithfully stayed in the church or denomination for years, finally coming to a point where they had to break away.

After further meditation and study on this topic, it led me to really question why the church has fallen short for so many? It came down to three key aspects that I think need real consideration if we want to truly live out our purpose as The Church.

First, there is a misconception about seeking God. If we are seeking God in a physical place, then we are looking in the wrong place. We do not need to invite God to be with us, He is already here. We need to step into His presence, because He is everywhere at all times. It is for us to recognize and choose Him. This can happen anywhere and we do not need to be in a church to do so. We have to understand that *we* are the Church, not a building!

Secondly, there is a huge chasm in biblical literacy. There are people attending churches every week of their lives and they have no idea what the Bible actually says. This is an epic shortfall of so many churches today. There is either no direct interaction with scripture by the congregation or the message is so watered down or even compromised, that congregants do not know what the truth actually is.

Lastly, there is not a consistent and sustained emphasis on the work of the Holy Spirit in the daily life of the believer. Believers are left powerless to fight the daily battles that are required to hold onto their faith. They have not been equipped properly by the church to make scripture applicable today with the power and authority of Jesus. Believers faithfully go to church, but they don't know what to do beyond that. This is the most vulnerable group. Many think they are saved and okay, but they carry-on like the rest of the world, making them an easy target for the enemy.

The above-mentioned principles are the fundamental tools of the faith, and they have been virtually non-existent in many churches. I believe it is because of these deficiencies that we are now seeing some of the outcomes in the world around us. And more importantly, why we are not seeing the next generation eager to stay within the faith.

We have to recognize The Church's role in the decline of today's society, especially as it relates to moral issues such as abortion, discrimination, sexual immorality issues, LGBT issues, increase in occult practices and forms of worship that are unbiblical. A recent Barna study revealed that only 36% of church leaders have a biblical worldview.[1] This is quite alarming. The

---

[1] https://www.arizonachristian.edu/2022/05/12/shocking-lack-of-biblical-worldview-among-american-pastors/

person who is leading the church is themselves not walking according to God's Word and Will. How then can the congregation live the faith, let alone carry on the faith properly or pass it to the next generation?

In order to really make any progress in this matter, it is essential to consider the following: *What is The Church? What is its role?* We will address the answers to these questions in detail in Chapter 3- Churches of Revelation. However, for now, we can look at what scripture commands us. In Matthew 28:16-20, Jesus tells us to go into the world (not stay in a building) make disciples and baptize. In 1 Timothy 5:3-16, Paul says true religion is the care of widows and orphans. According to Acts 2, we are also expected to be dedicated to teaching, fellowship and prayer. Do we see these attributes reflected in many of the modern-day churches?

Obviously, most of us are not in a position to change what is happening in our own church, let alone in every church. But that doesn't mean we stand still. In fact, it is quite the opposite.

This presents us with even more work to do. We need to fill the gap that The Church has left. This by no means implies that we are all expected to start some kind of ministry, unless that is what God is calling you to do. It does mean that we need to be more **Purposeful**, **Intentional** and **Explicit** in our faith, in every interaction and in every day of our lives. We need to walk in the Spirit and live according to scripture so others see it.

I first came across the acronym **PIE**[2] in my role as an educator. It is used as a guide for lesson planning in order to outline goals for the students. A good teacher will always make the content **P**urposeful, **I**ntentional and **E**xplicit for maximum access and comprehension for whatever is being taught. It has been the case many times that God has shown me how the things I encounter in my professional job can also inform His work and vice-versa. This led me to think about how this very essential understanding in education could make God's Word and Will clearer for the Church.

---

[2]https://www.languagemagazine.com/internetedition/langmag_pages/ProvidingDirect_LM07.pdf

I started to see the pieces so clearly fall together and scriptures were confirming this fact. It quickly became a cohesive model for understanding the nature of who we are and the work God has for us.

First is **Purpose**. Since the beginning of time, humans have been on a mission to find purpose. It seems even more true now since we have an entire generation of youth seeking for purpose strongly, yet they have been so deceived and distracted that they are looking in all the wrong places. Contrary to what the world wants you to believe, God's purpose for each one of us is the **same**. We are to bring glory to God and point others to Christ. That is it! That is our sole purpose. Humans have manipulated God's purpose for us because of our own fleshly desires. It is not about us and it never has been. It is always and only about Him!

To be clear, this is completely separate from the unique role we play in achieving this purpose. This is where God has created each of us as individuals with unique talents, gifts and callings. So, no matter what our role is or what we are called to do, our purpose is the same as mentioned above. This makes things so much clearer. 1 Corinthians 10:31 says, *"So whether you eat or drink or whatever you do, do it all for the glory of God."* We should not just be pursuing God in the big things, but the small everyday things as well.

So, living life purposefully means living to glorify God and serve His purpose! Anything else would be considered by Solomon to be vanity. Society has led us to believe that we are here to be rich, be powerful, be successful and to even be liked. Jesus was not rich, not liked and would not have been considered successful by earthly standards. But he was the embodiment of Purpose. He had one sole purpose, to glorify God, which He carried out to perfection with His own life. Jesus did nothing apart from what The Father told Him. He is our example and we should desire to become more like Him each day.

Now, onto **Intention**. Intentionality is connected to our very being. It is our identity. Here again, the world has been on a mission to hijack our identity. This has specifically been their objective for the current generation of youth. This can clearly be seen as in the fact that the world and its representatives cannot even define the difference between a man and a woman.

As this is being written, there are currently over 100 accepted genders and more are being added daily by the LGBTQ+++ community. This defies the facts of science known and accepted for thousands of years and the fact that Genesis 1:27 tells us that *God created us in His own image, male and female.*

Why is it so important to the enemy that we question our identity? Because then we are distracted from the fact that our identity is in Christ, which is where all that God has for us comes from. Satan knows we can be a terrible threat to him and fears that we will come to understand that. This is why the agenda of the world is so strong to tear us down at the level of identity. It makes us want to question everything, especially who we are.

Paul tells us in Acts 17:27-28, that God did this (created us) so that *we would seek him and* *perhaps reach out for him and find him, though he is not far from any one of us. **28** 'For in him we live and move and have our being".* We are nothing apart from Him. Therefore, living intentionally means we accept and walk in our identity in Christ. That means each day we arise for the day ahead knowing who Jesus is and how He is working in our lives through the Holy Spirit. When we understand this, we make different choices, have different desires and become set-apart from this world.

Finally, we have ***Explicit.*** Being explicit takes a conscious effort to live a lifestyle of excellence that is in alignment with God's Word and Will. This is the part that others see in us. They notice we are different. They watch how we speak, act and respond to the world around us, leading others to see we have an integrity that they do not often encounter in others. This is how we reflect the light of Christ in our own life. This is how we demonstrate that we have made a commitment to Christ and we weigh each decision and choice by this belief. Not only does this allow us to experience the favor of God in our life, but it also gives us an opportunity to share the Gospel as others come to trust us. Most importantly, this is what has an impact! It is not what we say, but how we live.

Being bold, explicit and unashamed to live out our faith, even against any pressures of society, is what will allow us it to pass it along to the next generation. This is where the true meaning of life comes from: being grounded in our belief and walking in it daily.

We need to consider ourselves teachers of the faith in whatever sphere of influence we have been placed in. This does not mean we need to teach lessons or even give fancy speeches, but we must live out our faith in a way that is **Purposeful**, **Intentional** and **Explicit,** so that others see Christ in us, have access to Him and will understand who He is and why we need Him.

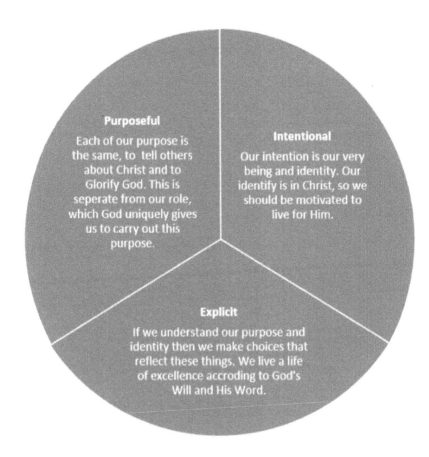

Purposeful

Each of our purpose is the same, to tell others about Christ and to Glorify God. This is seperate from our role, which God uniquely gives us to carry out this purpose.

Intentional

Our intention is our very being and identity. Our identify is in Christ, so we should be motivated to live for Him.

Explicit

If we understand our purpose and identity then we make choices that reflect these things. We live a life of excellence accroding to God's Will and His Word.

Once we understand this in the context of our own lives, then we can begin to share and have influence over others. Since the focus of this book is on reaching the next generation, those who we will want to have influence over are the youth. This is often easiest to do with those who have been placed in our care, such as our children and grandchildren.

Any well-intentioned caregiver looks after the needs of their children. We make sure they are fed properly and given all the basic needs. As the children are running out of the door on their way to school or play, we ask them, "Did you brush your teeth? Have you combed your hair? Did you put on a clean shirt? Have you had something to eat?" Jesus says in Matthew 6:25, *"Therefore I tell you, do not worry about your life, what you will eat or drink; or about your body, what you will wear. Isn't life more than food, and the body more than clothes?"* Therefore, as the children are running for the door, we should be asking, "Have you prayed today? Did you put on your Armor? What scripture have you consumed today?" We should be making conversations like this normal in our homes so that the children begin to develop their own sense of **PIE** in their faith from an early age.

Biblical literacy is going to be key in building this foundation for the next generation. At the start of education in America, literacy was developed through the reading of scripture. The Bible was used as a tool to teach everyone to learn how to read. Over time, other books began to be used in place of it, but the Bible was still integral in the home and part of most church services at the time. Therefore, it gave those generations the ability to memorize scripture and keep it close at hand. We know that the Word of God is the Sword in the Armor. It is what we need to defend ourselves against the enemy. How convenient then for Satan that there had been a steady decline of God and scripture in schools until 1962, when prayer and all references to God were considered to be unconstitutional and removed completely? It is interesting to note that since these decisions were made, not only has there been a moral decline in society, but also an overall decline in academics and literacy. This is because it all starts with God!

It is difficult to take a stand for faith and back up what you believe if you do not know what scripture says. We need to be in pursuit of biblical truth and not allow any compromise with the Word of God. It is not enough to read The Word daily. It is for us to meditate on it day and night and study it for all matters.

In the end, we can only change and control ourselves. So, we need to be sure that we are walking a righteous life, and in that walk, others will take notice. That then gives us the opportunity to share with others how Jesus has transformed us.

*These are the commands, decrees and laws
the* LORD *your God directed me to teach you to
observe in the land that you are crossing the
Jordan to possess, ² so that you, your children and
their children after them may fear the* LORD *your
God as long as you live by keeping all his decrees
and commands that I give you, and so that you
may enjoy long life. ³ Hear, Israel, and be careful to
obey so that it may go well with you and that you
may increase greatly in a land flowing with milk and
honey, just as the* LORD, *the God of your ancestors,
promised you.*

⁴ Hear, O Israel: The LORD *our God, the* LORD *is
one. ⁵ Love the* LORD *your God with all your
heart and with all your soul and with all your
strength. ⁶ These commandments that I give you
today are to be on your hearts. ⁷ Impress them on
your children. Talk about them when you sit at
home and when you walk along the road, when you
lie down and when you get up. ⁸ Tie them as
symbols on your hands and bind them on your
foreheads. ⁹ Write them on the doorframes of your
houses and on your gates.*

Deuteronomy 6:1-9

Thinking Generationally

*He decreed statutes for Jacob and established the law in Israel, which he commanded our ancestors to teach their children, **6** so the next generation would know them, even the children yet to be born, and they in turn would tell their children. **7** Then they would put their trust in God And would not forget his deeds but would keep his commands. **8** They would not be like their ancestors—a stubborn and rebellious generation, whose hearts were not loyal to God, whose spirits were not faithful to him.*

Psalm 78:5-8

One thing I can recall from an early age was how much my family loved Jesus. I did not glean this because we were regular church-goers. As a matter of fact, my father barely attended church unless it was for a family function. Rather this was because the name and reference of Jesus was ever present in my home. We did, however, regularly attend Sunday School where we heard scripture firsthand, but it was at home where we watched biblical principles play out. I grew up in a multi-generational home, which I understand is less common today. It was the case that my grandparents, aunt, uncle and parents were all within one building. This alone was instrumental in passing along a legacy of faith. All the adults in the environment had a direct impact on the youth in the home. The fact that the children saw others living out their faith daily spoke volumes. It was not that we were being read Bible stories at bedtime, but we got to see the real working-out of faith in both good, and even more so, difficult moments of life.

Building a legacy of faith requires conscious effort as described in Psalm 78. The statutes and works of the Lord need to be told to the next generation so they will learn to trust in God in their own right. I believe this is not just from talking the talk but walking the walk. It is the case that most of the really important lessons in life are caught, not taught. Therefore, we need to be sure that we allow children to see us working out our faith in the day-to-day walk of life. The more of these types of influences are in a child's life, the more demonstration of faith they will experience which will reinforce the foundations set at home.

One important consideration to this is if your child is going to school outside the home, we need to be aware that for 7 to 8 hours a day, they are being influenced by someone other than you. This has a significant impact on how they develop and how they view the world. Be careful not to be deceived in the fact that schools are labeled as public education. The reality is that it is government education and it has a clear agenda and worldview, which is not aligned to scriptural views in any manner. They will get from the education what the government deems important. While it is most likely not possible for each of us to homeschool our children, I encourage you to do so if you can. Either way, we need to understand that no matter where our children are schooled, we need to be the ones who's educating them.

Scripture tells us that fear of the Lord is the beginning of knowledge (Proverbs 9:10). We need to use God's Word as the foundation for educating our children. This needs to be the focus and the foundation of all things. God's Word is what will stay with the children no matter where they are. We also know from scripture that if we raise the child in the way they should go, they will not depart from it when they are old (Proverbs 22:6). This doesn't mean that they won't take a detour at some point, but God has His hand on them and will redirect them back.

Consider the common African Proverb, "It takes a village..." This means that an entire community is needed to raise a child who will reflect the values of that community when they are grown. Each person in that community contributes something to the benefit of the child's development. If this is true for raising a single child, how much more so is it for raising an entire generation? Remember, God speaks to generations!

Society and the government-run schools think they are the village your child should be raised by. However, according to God, The Church is called to be this village. It is the community of believers that are responsible for raising the next generation and advancing the Kingdom. God intended His people to work together to ensure that His law and statutes are followed for generations to come.

We are currently seeing the impact of what happens when we drop the baton of our responsibilities as The Church. We, as a village, have failed to pass along a solid Christian worldview and Chrisitan lifestyle to the next generation. It comes down to the fruits! The apple doesn't fall far from the tree. Children will tend to imitate a lifestyle that they were raised in. The trouble with this is that they can imitate positive or negative behaviors and choices. What are our children and grandchildren seeing us do? We need to be living by example and walking in faith and righteousness ourselves if we want our children to follow us. This is true inside church, but even more important in our daily life.

As described at the beginning of this chapter, the key influence may not be church attendance itself, but rather the impact of being consistently around a community of believers, which has a definite impact on the shaping of the individual's worldview. Specifically if the children are schooled in the government schools, they need a place to engage with those who aim to act based on biblical principles to counterbalance the time they spend with those who do not. Scripture tells us that we should gather as believers to edify and encourage one another.

With that being said, it is the case that church attendance has dropped at an alarming rate over the last few generations. It was typical for many in previous generations that, regardless of one's level of spiritual maturity, there was a reverence for God that resulted in attending church. This drop is not always intentional and it is certainly not true for all believers, but it's true for enough of those who proclaim to be Christians that it has tipped the scales against us.

One way I have seen this best described is by what is called the '4 Generation Fade', coined by Shane Pruitt, a well known Evangelist.[3] He describes it as such:

Generation 1: Parents don't make church a high priority for their kids.

Generation 2: Those kids grow up and make church less of a priority for their kids.

Generation 3: Those kids grow up and make church no priority for their kids.

Generation 4: Those kids grow up without a biblical knowledge of God.

Since it is a fade, this takes time and the impact is not necessarily immediate. So, what is the long-term impact? Besides children who do not know who God is, they also do not know who they are. We have an entire generation of youth who are godless, without identity, and in many cases without a biblically defined family. We can look at all sorts of excuses for the ills of society that have

---

[3] Shane Pruitt- https://twitter.com/shane_pruitt78/status/1402707285785333 761

brought us here. But if we truly want to change course, we must look closely at ourselves as individuals and as believers and take some of the blame. We need to repent and get back to doing the work of the Kingdom.

One aspect that is essential in addressing this fade is our resolve for standing firm. We must not compromise the faith that we are intending to pass along to the next generation. We need to be sure we are presenting the true Gospel in an uncompromised manner. It must be clear to all around us what we believe and the line that we will not cross. While we always want to engage others with integrity and compassion, that does not mean we weaken our position in standing for what matters. These types of changes are progressive and happen over time through a slippery slope of complacency, coalescence and compromise with the world.

The best analogy for this is from the famous musical, *Fiddler on the Roof*. The entire story basically addresses the very topic of this book.

The main character, Tavia, is a devout Jewish Father who wants to keep the faith and family tradition alive for his daughters amongst a quickly changing society. It is customary within their religion for matches to be made for marriages even from an early age, particularly when the family is of meeker standing. However, Tavia loves his daughters immensely and cares about their feelings. He does not want them to be mismatched and unhappy for the rest of their life. The point here is that the eldest daughter breaks tradition and makes her own match with a boy who she has been friends with her entire life. Tavia, against his better judgment, consents because even though this was unorthodox for the match to be made this way, the person was a good fit for his daughter and he is of the same faith.

When it comes time for the second daughter to marry, she doesn't even ask for permission. She tells Tavia that she will be married to someone who isn't orthodox in his faith. She does, however, want the father's blessing for the union. Tavia concedes again and gives them the blessing because they seem to be in love.

Finally, the last daughter goes behind his back and marries someone completely outside the faith. In the Jewish custom, this child would need to be disowned because they have turned from God and their faith. So, in essence, one compromise allowed for another more greater, and then another even more so. This is what has happened in the generational slide we see today. Obviously in this case, it is not only the issue of marriage, but a general slide from standing for the values of God's Word in everyday matters, to going along with the world in order to get along.

We do not want our children and grandchildren to become a statistic. A recent Barna study says that 59% of teens will disconnect from the church even though they were raised in it.[4] We have been preaching and teaching from one generation to the next, but are we reaching them? This has a far lasting impact. When we are not

---

[4] https://www.barna.com/research/church-attendance-2022/

living the way God has called us, with the power of the Holy Spirit, we have no influence over those who do not know God yet. We cannot convince anyone of anything because they do not see it in us!

We need to be sure to have a voice and influence over the lives of our children. There are so many worldly "experts" that are redefining the role of parents to be more of a contemporary or friend to their child. This is misguided and not supported at all as the role given to us as parents according to scripture. We need to take a stand for parent's rights to be able to raise our children according to God's Word. We also need to acknowledge that with this role comes tremendous responsibility to ensure that we are doing what God's Word actually says in the raising of our children.

When we recognize God as our Father, then we can realize that He is the ultimate parent. The most important thing we can do in our role as a parent is to model from how God parents us.

God loves us, guides us and rebukes us. God is for us and works all things out for our good. Our children need to trust us and know that we are for them, just as God is for us. So, when everything else around them falls apart, they know that no matter what, we will comfort and correct them. They need to trust that we will tell them the truth while still loving them unconditionally. They need to feel comfortable to come to us for advice and know that we will guide their path back on course, with the help of God.

We cannot be 'sideline parents'. We need to connect to and engage with our children in meaningful ways daily. This is what is required in any good relationship. We need to build open lines of communication so they can trust us above all else, because we are trusting God above all else. This is probably the most difficult part. We may not always be speaking to them about what is popular or in the way that other parents are to their children, but that doesn't matter. We need to take the role of parent as God has defined it and speak the truth to our children in love and in a developmentally appropriate manner.

Feelings may be hurt along the way, but God will repair what has been broken if we are obedient to Him. We need to commit to stand on God's Word for every decision being made in the home. Doing otherwise is disastrous.

The outcome of not building such relationships is evident in another common, but lesser-known, African Proverb that may be far more powerful than the one introduced earlier. It states, "The child who is not embraced by the village will burn it down to feel its warmth". This implies that when a child is not raised-up and guided in love and truth by the family unit and community of believers in a meaningful way, he or she will rebel against it. Children benefit from rules and parameters. We do not need to impose ridiculous restrictions on our children, we just need to enforce the rules that God has given us. This creates meaning, purpose and value in life so that a child feels embraced and confident in their role and identity according to God. This is how they will withstand the landmines of the world today.

Now thinking beyond the walls of our home, who are the influences in our children's and grandchildren's' lives? This brings us to another major change we have seen over time which is the loss of multi-generational households. This concept goes back to biblical times. New couples did not generally move geographically too far from their families and communities. However today, living in a global world, it is quite possible that grandchildren do not even know who their grandparents are, let alone get the benefit of hearing their stories and feeling their love. There is definitely an artificial severing of the generational link due to this.

Now there may not be much that can be done in terms of bringing this back, but then we need to consider how to fill the void of this loss. And it is a loss. In a multi-generational home, there is a sense of security and stability when multiple generations cohabitate in one location. From a child's perspective, they know someone will always be there. This is where life's lessons are worked out.

There doesn't need to be so much of a formal instruction, but children learn by example. They see how family members responded to life's ups and downs. This allows for testimonies and stories of God's faithfulness in that family's lineage to be shared and used for the building of future faith. Be encouraged. Even when children are not listening, they are hearing. Keep preaching, keep sharing and keep praying over your children. The Lord hears and this is covering them more than you know. When it really matters, the Holy Spirit will bring all the words and prayers for your children back to life in their spirit.

In today's society we have children as young as six weeks old being sent to daycare to be raised by a total stranger. Most people are unaware of the daycare person's moral character or the character of the multitude of other children within the facility they are spending 7-8 hours a day in. The fact is, **these** are the people who are raising the children. Now understandably, some people truly have no choice in making a decision such as this, but that does not negate the responsibility of the parents to still be sure that the influences otherwise in the child's life are godly and that biblical values are solidly integrated at home.

Again, not to focus on how we got to this point, but it is important to understand the history so we do not repeat it. Another tactic of the enemy in this respect has been through the Feminist movement. He has successfully drawn the majority of mothers out of the home under the guise of it being in their best interests. This was sold as a virtuous movement because women should have the same rights as men. While it is true that our rights should be the same, it is clear from God's Word that women's roles are not the same as a man's.

The mother is the one who is responsible for raising and nurturing the children in all respects, including education. As soon as the enemy allowed a woman's desires to be fulfilled outside the home, this is when we began to lose the first generation of children. Satan knew that if women (mothers) had their eyes on other things, then they would not be able to keep their eyes on their children, and this is precisely how Satan swooped in and hijacked an entire generation and multiple generations thereafter. Now we are in a battle to rescue them back for the Kingdom. Reestablishing the biblical role of family is needed if we are to reverse all that Satan has stolen from us.

Scripture repeats multiple times that blessings and punishments are handed-down until the 3rd and 4th generations. Exodus 34:6-7 tells us that *God has endless mercy for those He loves, but he will not let the guilty go unpunished.* God says that *children are punished for the sins of their parents.* When a generation follows God, they receive the blessings of God. This in turn passes on to their children after them. When a generation falls away from God, it brings on a punishment, which will also be inherited by the next generation. Sometimes the judgment will come directly from God as is the case in Exodus, while other times, the judgment is simply the result of the consequences caused by the disobedience. Either way, our dependence is on God's mercy and our Hope is in Jesus. God, willing in His mercy, He will allow us to turn back to Him and rebuild once again to repair our relationship and re-establish His blessings.

Since God thinks generationally, then we should too. Embracing remembrance and sharing what God has done preserves the faith for the next generation. Afterall someone first passed it down to us. We should feel compelled to share the goodness of God and His faithfulness throughout the generations. Psalm 78:1-4 reminds us, *"My people, hear my teaching; listen to the words of my mouth 2 I will open my mouth with a parable; I will utter hidden things, things from old— 3 things we have heard and known, things our ancestors have told us. 4 We will not hide them from their descendants; we will tell the next generation the praiseworthy deeds of the LORD, his power, and the wonders he has done."* This is a conscious and thoughtful effort to make the name of the Lord known for generations. God works in patterns and cycles. We can see this reflected overtime in history as well. Thinking generationally can be grounded in knowing and studying patterns of society throughout history.

Relating back to Shane Pruitt's 4 Generation Slide, there is something else historically significant about the 4th generation. Based on the research of William Strauss and Neil Howe, they propose a theory that there are four generational cycles, each lasting about 20-25 years. They suggest that at the end of the fourth generational cycle there appears to be a major societal shift.[5] While this theory is not predictive, the general pattern of history would support their findings. In essence, this aligns with scripture about how God uses the different generational periods for His purpose, to teach His lessons. Strauss and Howe's theory is as follows:

The First Turning (The High): This period of time is characterized by strength and unity. Since it is a time that follows a crisis, there is a sense of obligation to unite and rebuild what had been damaged or lost. People are eager to work

---

[5] https://www.fourthturning.com/

together and support one another for the common good.

The Second Turning (The Awakening): After a period of unity, society often moves more towards individualism. During this second turning, most people desire to achieve their own goals and vision. This is a time for questioning societal norms and institutions. People feel empowered to make changes based on their own perspectives.

The Third Turning (The Unraveling): This period is characterized by a mistrust in others as a whole and specifically those in authority. People begin to separate more and more based on ideology. Freedom and personal rights become a focus for division within society.

The Fourth Turning (The Crisis): This period marks the end of the cycle and is characterized by a major crisis. There is a shaking that causes a major shift in thinking and a need to put all emphasis towards the crisis. Ultimately, this ends in the reshaping of society and then the cycle begins again.

In fact, you can find that this exact "Fourth Turning" cycle continues to repeat itself throughout the Old Testament in the stories of the Israelites' triumphs and their disobediences. It's easiest to see this cycle at work starting in the Second Turning. The awakening this generation experiences begins the transition from the First Turning's unity and peace into division. This time plants the seeds for a new vision of individuality and pursuing a road forward undefined by the previous generations' institutions.

This is fertile soil for the Third Turning's unraveling, in which we see the Israelites complete apostasy. It is marked by their creation of idols, distrust in others, and fragmentation. This leads to the Fourth Turning, the crisis, in which God judges his people. This process of judgment bleeds into the First Turning as the Israelites repent, overcome their punishment, and are brought into a new high. Once we have arrived again at the First Turning, we find that community is strong, trust in God is paramount, and peace is restored. Unfortunately, this cyclical story teaches us that peace will not last forever, and soon enough the next generation will awaken the Second Turning once more.

The underlying characteristic of this cycle or these turnings is the fact that once a generation chooses to become disobedient to God, there is unrest, decline and chaos. It is for that generation to recognize the cause of the strife and to move forward to bring about the next turning. Recognition and repentance are essential. God's people (the Church) need to earnestly put Him back as the center of all things. Then God can rightfully deal with our disobedience and restore what was lost.

Walking alongside those who come after us is essential for passing on the faith. We want to engage with, encourage and guide those in the next generation to stand firm and carry their faith forward. Let us make the most of opportunities to mentor and build relationships with the youth in our spheres of influence. If we notice a gap in one of their circles, let's pray for them and be the one to help bridge that gap by introducing them to Jesus.

Disobedience and Defeat of Israel

The people served the LORD throughout the lifetime of Joshua and of the elders who outlived him and who had seen all the great things the LORD had done for Israel.

8 Joshua son of Nun, the servant of the LORD, died at the age of a hundred and ten. *9* And they buried him in the land of his inheritance, at Timnath Heres in the hill country of Ephraim, north of Mount Gaash.

10 After that whole generation had been gathered to their ancestors, another generation grew up who knew neither the LORD nor what he had done for Israel. *11* Then the Israelites did evil in the eyes of the LORD and served the Baals. *12* They forsook the LORD, the God of their ancestors, who had brought them out of Egypt. They followed and worshiped various gods of the peoples around them. They aroused the LORD's anger

Judges 2:7-12

The Churches of

Revelation

Since we are called to be The Church, we need to look to scripture for what God's perspective is about The Church. One of the greatest references for this can be found in the Book of Revelation, chapters 2 and 3. Specific messages are revealed to John for each of the major churches of the time. Each church is highlighted for what they were doing that was pleasing to the Lord and then told where they were falling short. If they heed the advice being given to them, it will result in God's ultimate reward.

We can learn so much from what is being revealed in the messages to these churches because we are The Church. If we want to have longevity and impact in faith, we need to consider what has been told to these end-time churches and apply the lessons to reap the benefits.

Therefore, the remainder of this book is organized into chapters inspired by the key words of advice given to each church. If we apply these instructions, we will be able to stand and leave a legacy of faith to be passed down until Christ comes again.

In Revelation, John is visited by Jesus with a specific message for seven specific churches. These are all churches of what was then considered The Asia Minor. They fell along the Aegean Sea, in what would now be considered modern-day Turkey. These churches were in close proximity to where John was writing from, on the Island of Patmos after he was exiled. While they are intended for these specific churches, they have relevance to The Church and to us as individuals.

Ephesus

Ephesus, the first church addressed, had worked hard for the faith and persevered against evil. However, they had lost their focus and their first love, Christ. They are told that they will lose their lampstand if they do not repent. This is significant because this means they lose their light and their favor from God. Love and light go together. We are drawn to light and therefore it shows prominence. When Jesus is our center and our focus, we radiate His light and therefore draw others to us, which means to Him. This allows us to fully display Christ's love for us and our love towards others.

Ephesus is told that if they are victorious, they will be able to eat from the Tree of Life. The Tree of Life is first mentioned in Genesis 2. It is mentioned after the Tree of Knowledge of Good and Evil, which is the tree that Adam and Eve ate from. After they disobeyed God by eating from this tree, God sent angels to protect the Tree of Life, so Adam and Eve could not gain access to it for their own protection.

The Tree of life represents God's goodness, mercy and eternal life. This is a symbol of God's reward for His people. Our reward for keeping Christ as our first love is eternal life and being in the presence of the fullness of God. So love, particularly for Christ but for others as well, as we are commanded to do, is essential in passing along the faith. If we have as our main objective to love others the way Jesus loved us, we can be successful in reaching those who are in darkness because love and light are magnetic.

Smyrna

Smyrna is the second church addressed in Revelation 2. It is not rebuked directly and they were told that they have withstood the suffering that they had been experiencing due to the increase in pagan influences around them. They are given advice to endure the suffering and not to have fear. The suffering will only be temporary, but the reward will be eternal. Smyrna is told that there will be persecution and some will be put in prison or even martyred for their faith, but they must endure. If they can be victorious in this, they will be awarded the crown of life and not experience the second death. This essentially means that if they remain faithful, then their spirit will automatically live for eternity.

The crown of life is referred to in other places of scripture. It speaks of this specifically in James 1:12, *"Blessed is the one who perseveres under trial because, having stood the test, that person will receive the crown of life that the Lord has promised to those who love him."* The crown of life represents ultimate victory. It is a gift from God for those who love Him. This is an eternal reward and we receive it when we do not give up!

We cannot give up while the next generation is under our watch. Although persecution may come, we must not fear and we must stand firm. This will cause us to have to make difficult choices and often suffer, but the reward for our endurance is promised and it is eternal. This means our efforts are not in vain. We can help guide the next generation and also secure our place in eternity. That is the ultimate reward!

Pergamos

Now we address the church that, in many ways, reflects the current status of the modern day church and was part of the impetus for the title of this book. Pergamos is told that it has severely compromised the truth of God's Word and has allowed paganism and idolatry to enter into the house of God. They are calling themselves believers, yet carrying-on in ungodly ways. They lost their integrity in the faith. Pergamos is specifically warned against their pagan practices and sexual immorality within the church.

Like today, we see so many New Age influences in church practice. There is also a strong movement of progressive Christianity as a way for the church to seem relevant and relatable to the demands of society. This has caused major compromise. So much so, that it often becomes an entirely different 'Christianity' altogether. In addition, we also witness outright blessings from some churches on same-sex unions. There are countless churches that fly LGBTQ+ flags, have openly homosexual pastors and hold same-sex marriage ceremonies. This is exactly what is being called-out by God in its response to Pergamos. Yet we, under our watch, are allowing it to happen here again.

Pergamos is warned that they must repent and give up their ungodly behavior. If they do not, God will fight them with the sword of His Mouth. This is a great judgment and we know it will not end favorably for the church. However, if they repent by changing their behaviors and aligning their doctrine to God's Word, they can become victorious. Their reward will be hidden manna and a white stone with a new name on it. These are symbols of God's provision, blessings and forgiveness.

Thyatira

Thyatira clearly had works of faith. They showed love and service to the church and the community. However, they were identified as an adulterous church because they allowed sexual immorality and idolatry to become acceptable in the church. Many had entertained Jezebel and regarded her as a prophetess. God threatens discipline and even death to Jezebel for luring the people into immorality and refusing to repent. He says that he will destroy all of her children.

Revelation 2:23 says that, "*God searches the hearts and minds*" of the people. In addition, verse 24 mentions that God addresses, '*the rest of you*', which tells us that not all of those in the church embraced the teaching of Jezebel. This shows discernment. While the church was being infiltrated by the' deep sins' of Satan, not all had fallen for the deception.

God promises to those who repent and do not fall under the spell of immorality, that they will have authority over the nations. Those who are steadfast until the end will rule and be given the morning star. This symbolizes authority and power.

Sardis

Sardis is addressed as the dead church. They looked alive to others because they had activity going on and the church had attendance, but they were just going through the motions. It was as if there was a front put up in their faith. This was due to their lack of reliance on the Holy Spirit. Sardis is told that their work is unfinished because they are not really walking and preaching the fullness of the Gospel. Sardis lacked the genuineness and authenticity in their faith to actually have impact.

They were ineffective in their mission because they lacked the Holy Spirit's guidance. They were working in the flesh and not the spirit. This led them to become a powerless church, which means they had no real impact for the Kingdom. Sardis is warned to wake up and gain strength and enliven the things that were lost and dead. If they repented and were successful, they would be clothed in white and have their name in the book of life. This symbolizes forgiveness and eternal life.

Philadelphia

Philadelphia was not given any correction, but rather they were given comfort. God saw their struggle to stay faithful and have strength during evil times. They were told that they had held to God's Word and kept His Name. Philadelphia has endured patiently and God was pleased with them. Since they were suffering then, God will not allow them to suffer in the end.

Laodicea

Laodicea is known as the luke-warm church. Of all the churches, Laodicea gets the harshest response from God. They have no commitment one way or the other. Because of this, God will 'spit them out of His mouth'. More importantly, they flaunt themselves as rich and righteous but they did not realize that they were pitiful, poor, blind and naked. Laodicea was deceived and living a compromised faith.

God rebukes their behavior because He loves them and God's desire is for them to repent and commit in full sincerity to Christ. If they were successful, they would sit at the throne with Christ.

It is worthwhile to mention that church is wherever Jesus is and where The Word of God is being applied. We are told to be doers of the Word, not just hearers. There is no mention of a necessity for a building. Early believers met in homes and then dispersed for missionary work from there. The characterization and the advice to each of these churches speak to what we see in many churches today. At some level, this can be an accurate characterization of an individual believer's behaviors as well.

Having reviewed the Churches of Revelation, it is important to note that all of the churches, with the exception of Philadelphia, had compromised in some way. They had become weakened in that they were no longer set apart from the rest of the world. Sadly, this is the state of the modern day Church as well. For many, the Church no longer holds a place of influence in the day-to-day lives of the believers. It has been relegated to something on the To-Do list on Sunday mornings. The Church must have an impact and influence on the world in a positive and biblical manner if we want to see change and strengthen the next generation of faith.

While the emphasis here has been specifically on the Churches of Revelation, it is important to note the overall shift in The Church in general from the 1st Century to Modern Day. It is really a stark contrast as seen in the chart below. We have really moved away from what we were called to do as The Church. We need to regain our focus and get back on the path of God's vision for us.

The Early Church	The Modern Church
• Led by Apostles	• Led by pastors
• Gathered Daily	• Gather once a week
• Focused on maturing the saints	• Focused on caring for the saints
• Discipleship	• Church membership
• Doctrinal Teaching	• Topic based teaching
• Theology	• Psychology
• Deliverance & transformation	• Counseling
• Missions focused	• In house focused
• Marked those who caused division & discord	• Pray & protect those who cause division & discord
• Strong emphasis on sending	• Strong emphasis on gathering

Sourced from The Narrow Path Facebook Community Group

It is the case that many churches have become more interested in filling seats than filling lives with truth. For the sake of being inclusive and in the interest of being liked by the world, they have compromised the integrity of scripture to make it more palatable for the general public. This has made them ineffective in making change and influencing the next generation for Christ.

The next generation does not need more religion or feel-good events, it needs biblical foundation, relationships and mentoring. There is a strong desire within this generation to be understood and related to. These relationships are built on trust and truth. We will not truly win anyone for the Kingdom when our doctrine does not align with God's Word. We shouldn't think that we need to wrap the Word of God in a shiny wrapper so others will accept Him. The Gospel and the fullness of Jesus is enough. Glitz and glamor are worldly mindsets and they do not produce long-lasting impact. This may get people into the door, but it will not make them stay. People need a genuine encounter with the Living God through the Holy Spirit. This only happens when there is truth at the center.

One aspect that has exacerbated this situation is the division and extremes within church beliefs. God is unique. He created us uniquely and we are all connected to God in our own way. Because of this fact, we are free to worship God how the Holy Spirit leads. However, as it relates to the doctrine of the church, it should not be so broad that it allows anything to be practiced if it doesn't align with scripture. We have seen such extremes between 'Christian' believers such as the fundamentalists, charismatics and progressivists. Not to mention all the 'offshoot' followings that are basically cults under the banner of Christianity.

These extremes are causing so many to fall through the cracks. When someone is truly seeking, they can become confused and distracted easily because the church cannot even agree on what they believe and where they truly stand on a multitude of issues. It leads many to question the integrity of the church, and then in turn, it makes them question God.

The Truth of God's Word should never be compromised. Doctrine is not based on opinion. It is based on biblical accuracy. Common Christian doctrine has been agreed on for centuries. The facts and foundations absolutely cannot change in order to suit the whims of society. If it does, this undermines the role of The Church and the authority of scripture.

This division is further marked by the dichotomy of individual believers within the Church amongst the passive and dominant believers. The completely passive believer becomes an ineffective Christian who exhibits no influence on culture. In contrast is the dominant believer who is power-hungry and wants to 'minister' everywhere but serves no one but themselves. Often the emphasis for the dominant Christian is on this life more so than the next.

The passive Christians are the believers who go to church on Sunday out of obligation but do not bring anything about the faith outside the four walls of the church itself. This cannot impact the next generation. It says in scripture that we are compelled to share our testimony and the Gospel (1 Corinthians 9:16). Scripture also tells us to make the most of every opportunity (Ephesians 5:15-17) and to engage wisely with those outside the faith (Colossians 4:5). Our faith needs to be seen in us so it points others to Christ.

We cannot keep our faith in a box. Sometimes this simply means that we are to live our faith within the context of our own lives. Other times this means we need to be involved in things that are bigger than us. For example, community relations, school boards, local government and so on. If there aren't believers in the larger segments of the day-to-day world, we will not have influence over it.

Every person in every position has an agenda. The world has made plain what their agenda is and it is not godly. We must stand in the gap and represent the biblical worldview in every sphere of influence that impacts our lives. We cannot just sit back and wait for God to act. That is why he created us; so we can move the Kingdom forward. We need to speak truth, influence change and make God known to the rest of the world! This does not happen from a church pew on Sundays or from our living rooms. We need to engage and put ourselves out there for the Kingdom.

On the other hand, there are the dominant Christians who are 'on-fire' for God, but they only serve in a manner that serves themselves. Often this comes with the need to be liked or validated by others. This is like poison to the faith because its pursuit is for power, prosperity or personal gain. None of these things will impact the next generation either because it is not authentic and it is not for the Kingdom, but rather for self. True ministry is selfless. Although God will bless us for it, that should not be the reason we do it. Scripture tells us that whatever we do, we are to do it for the Lord rather than for man (Colossians 3:23).

We are called to be salt and light in the world. We cannot add flavor to our surroundings if we do not interact with others in a godly way. We also cannot be a beacon if we are hidden in our home. We must go into the world and do so on the authority of Christ and for the glory of God.

Lastly, let's be mindful of the 'churches' that have gone off the rails. Those churches that have become territorial, divisive and carnal, directing their focus on money, miracles, entertainment, pastors or on ministry passion, but not on God! The Churches of Ephesus and Pergamos were warned about this. They became distracted by idols and the world, therefore losing their first love and focus. When those who are seeking God and direction witness the dysfunction of these types of churches, it hurts all of us as believers, but also blemishes God's reputation.

In the wake of this dysfunction are millions of spiritual casualties, those who have stepped away from the faith due to being hurt and confused by The Church. In some cases, these souls will find other ways to connect to God, but for others they may be lost to the faith forever. It is absolutely critical that in these end-times that we be the end-time church that God is looking for. This will happen when we take heed of the warnings and advice spelled out clearly in Revelation. Let us love deeply, have perseverance, show integrity, use discernment, display authenticity, depend on God's strength and fully commit to Christ in our own lives.

We believe strongly that these attributes that are revealed to these churches by God are necessary to help build up the modern church and pass along our faith to the next generation. We are indeed in different times and need a different approach for how to reach the next generation for

Christ, but there is no better direction to follow than the guidance given by God Himself. He demands love, endurance, integrity, discernment, authenticity, patience, and commitment from His Church. To that end, you will see that the remaining chapters in this book address each one of these words of advice in detail and explore the application of how this can impact the next generation of faith. These are important aspects to reflect upon as individuals and as The Church.

Love

Do everything in love.

1 Corinthians 16:14

The message to the church of Ephesus is that they had lost their first love (Revelation 2:1-7). This refers to the fact that they were doing 'church' functions but had forgotten that this was being done for Christ Himself. They were working hard and trying to adhere to doctrine, but they lost their dedication. They lacked the love and purpose for why they were doing it. It is not coincidental that this is the first of the churches addressed. It is from love that everything else will flow. Love is one of the strongest forces and motivational factors in life. It is because of love that God created us. It is because of love that Christ died for us. It is because of love that we should have compassion for one another. Love is the glue that is holding it all together.

In 1 Corinthians 16:14, Paul is writing about the mission work of going out to spread the Gospel. He is encouraging the church to stand firm in faith and be bold, but most of all, do everything in love. We are going to face opposition, differences in opinion and views. This is to be expected. How we approach these differences is the key to our effectiveness. Love is what allows us to build relationships.

For most of us we have heard the word love all our lives, from our friends and family, in books and movies, in talks about things we enjoy, but because this word has been used so casually, it has lost its effect. In addition, there has been a steady redefining of the word *love* over the past several generations, starting in the 1960s.

While the counterculture movement of the Hippies initially started as anti-war and anti-government, the theme of love was woven into each argument. They protested on the grounds of love and peace. While they also desired to move away from materialism, this movement turned its outward desires onto self, where love was for self and doing what felt good for the individual. This segwayed perfectly into the sexual revolution movement, where ultimately the idea of love was expressed through sex.

Similarly, we find ourselves today in the 'love is love' movement. This is characterized by tolerance, acceptance and validity given to any individual's desires for love in any manner with any person or thing. This has opened the gates for some unnatural and ungodly things, such as pedophilia, homosexual unions, and bestiality, all causing a perversion to the very essence of love. With this redefinition of the word, there is no end to the possible interpretations of this. There was a news article recently, quoting a middle-aged woman who says she is "ecosexual", and is in a love relationship with a tree.[6]

It is clear that society's definition of love is not the same as the love spoken of in scripture. It is not merely about sexuality, or feeling good about yourself, or an object of affection or even a

---

[6] https://nypost.com/2023/12/26/lifestyle/ecosexual-woman-claims-shes-in-love-with-oak-tree/

temporal platitude. Rather, love is sacrifice, love is commitment, love is compassion. Love and compassion moved Jesus to heal others. Love moved Christ to look beyond the cross. Love is the foundational component for anything of value. Satan knows this fact also, which is why he has once again manipulated the language and meaning around God's Intention for love.

With the challenges discussed in the generational divide in a previous chapter, it has led to so many broken families, relationships and people. This generation is hurting and confused in so many ways. Our society has fallen into a trap of wanting to be liked by everyone. As a result, there is a need to affirm everyone's opinions, feelings and identity. However, this has been done at the expense of being honest and truthful. So in essence, we have traded love for likes.

Empathy is the ability to understand and share in another person's feelings. While empathy is important to display compassion in the sense of understanding others, it can lead down a slippery slope of sin when given into. This causes us to make judgments with our emotions rather than our wisdom and discernment. Comforting someone who is living in an immoral way because we want to be empathetic does not show that we love them. It says that we want to be liked by them. So, we will say what makes them feel better, but it may not result in a change of behavior. In addition, this empathy can mislead and drag us into the weeds with this person. That will not help us or them.

Love is a need. It is a basic need for everyone. We have been created in such a way so we would seek the truest form of it in our relationship with God. Love is what draws us near to Him, however, even secular sources identify the necessity for love. For instance, in a popular humanistic psychology framework known as *Maslow's Hierarchy of Needs*[7], love is placed right at the center of the model. This is because it is a central factor in our development as an individual, as well as for building strong relationships with others. However, we do not need to rest in man's wisdom when there are multitudes of scriptures that speak

---

[7] https://www.simplypsychology.org/maslow.html

about love. 1 John 4:19 tells us, *"we love because He first loved us."*

Maslow's hierarchy of needs

One of the most well-known scriptural references for love is 1 Corinthians 13. Verses 4-7 state, *"Love is patient, love is kind. It does not envy, it does not boast, it is not proud. 5 It does not dishonor others, it is not self-seeking, it is not easily angered, it keeps no record of wrongs. 6 Love does not delight in evil but rejoices with the truth. 7 It always protects, always trusts, always hopes, always perseveres."* These verses are read at most every wedding and are often quoted when speaking about this topic. It concludes with verse 13, *"And now these three remain: faith, hope and love. But the greatest of these is love."*

Upon deeper reflection there are subtleties about how God views love and just how powerful love truly is. Below is a wonderful chart from an article published by Bethany Christian Services Organization[8], detailing what love embraces and what love resists. This encapsulates the fact that just because we love, or say we love, it doesn't mean we accept all things.

Love embraces	Love resists
Patience (is patient)	Envy (isn't envious)
Kindness (is kind)	Boasting (isn't boastful)
Truth (rejoices with the truth)	Arrogance (isn't arrogant)
Resilience (bears all things)	Rudeness (isn't rude)
Faith (believes all things)	Selfishness (doesn't insist on its own way)
Hope (hopes all things)	Anger (isn't irritable)
Endurance (endures all things)	Resentment (isn't resentful)
Perseverance (never fails)	Wrongdoing (doesn't rejoice in wrongdoing)

Another common verse says "love thy neighbor" (Leviticus 19:18). The question is, who is

---

[8] https://bethany.org/resources/love-embraces-and-resists

our neighbor? The answer is not just those in our community, but everyone we meet. This is how Jesus approached each person He encountered, even those who were difficult to love. This is because Jesus did not look at people and wonder what they could do for Him. He was thinking *what could he do for them?* Our heart has to want to reach out to others, no matter what the circumstances are.

Jesus said others will know us by our love. So, the way we reach the next generation is first to love them as Christ loves us all. This cannot be superficial but actual in that we can see beyond whatever our differences of opinion or beliefs might be. We need to meet them where they are and reach into their circumstances and hurt. But just as Jesus did, it is not for us to leave them where they are but to help them make corrections to where they have gone astray. God rebukes and corrects those He loves. This is not in a scolding manner of any sorts, but in an embrace and genuine concern for their well-being. This starts with telling them the truth, since this will most likely be the opposite of what the world has been telling them for far too long.

Love is truth. This means telling the truth even when it is difficult. If you truly love someone, you would not want them deceived and you would want them to know the truth so they can make good choices. We are not called to judge, but we are told to correct what is unrighteous. We can only be effective in doing this when we speak the truth in love (Ephesians 4:15).

Speaking the truth in love requires communication. Therefore, opening lines of communication between the generations is essential. We need to create spaces where real and difficult conversations can be had without the fear of judgment. Here again, this will most likely not take place within the walls of a church because others may not enter such a place. We need to think about the reach we can have in the places where the next generation is engaged, such as parks, college campuses, sporting events and concerts. If God opens-up opportunities for us in these places, we should take the leap of faith to reach out. However, start wherever you are. This could be with your own grandchildren or your neighbor's children. Be present and be available to share Christ's love wherever He calls you.

Love is listening. Oftentimes, listening is even more important than what we say. We need to really hear others in their hurt and need and be able to set aside our feelings or preconceived notions and really listen to those who are reaching out. Listening builds trust and trust builds relationships. If we show we have taken the time to listen, it conveys that they are being loved. This creates opportunities to stretch beyond ourselves and share the love of Christ.

Love is forgiveness. We are told over and over again in scripture how important forgiveness is. Deep inside we know this is the right thing to do, but often it is also very difficult. Forgiveness of others demonstrates a heart like Jesus, expressing selfless love. 1 Peter 4:8 says, *"Above all, love each other deeply, because love covers over a multitude of sins."*

Forgiveness is not just important for the other person, but it is important for us as well. It heals us and brings us in closer union with Christ. Mark 11:25 tells us that if we are to approach God in prayer, we should forgive others first. Then God will hear us and forgive us as well. Similarly, Jesus said to forgive 70 times 7 against anyone who has hurt us (Matthew 18:21-35).

It is because we are loved and forgiven by Our Father that we are required to do the same for others. Love and forgiveness go hand-in-hand. If we are holding onto something that is preventing us from reaching out to someone for Christ, we need to pray for the release of this so God can work through us and in us. This is how we keep the unity of faith. *"Therefore, as God's chosen people, holy and dearly loved, clothe yourselves with compassion, kindness, humility, gentleness and patience. 13 Bear with each other and forgive one another if any of you has a grievance against someone. Forgive as the Lord forgave you. 14 And over all these virtues put on love, which binds them all together in perfect unity* (Colossians 3:12-14).

Perseverance

You need to persevere so that when you have done the will of God, you will receive what he has promised.

Hebrews 10:36

Recalling again the nature of God's perspective being focused on eternity, the here and now is just a blip on the screen of the bigger picture. In order to win faith for generations, we have to have a long-term perspective in mind. This takes endurance and perseverance.

Endurance is defined as the ability to suffer or sacrifice short-term pain to receive a reward that has long-term gain. This is the stamina to keep fighting the good fight, even in the midst of struggle and persecution.

Perseverance is having persistence in doing something regardless of delay or difficulty. While these two concepts are similar in nature, they are independent and both necessary if we are Kingdom-minded. We need to be willing to go the distance for Jesus.

Jesus warned us that we would have challenges in this world (John 16:33). He also told us that we would be persecuted for his name-sake (Matthew 10:22). Yet, God promised to never leave or forsake us (Deuteronomy 31:8) and that He is with us until the very end (Matthew 28:20). This should give us confidence to move forward and share our faith even in difficult situations. We are not acting alone and we are not working our own will, but the Will of God. Surely, He will see to all of the details. We just need to show up! God is looking for willing people who trust Him and move according to His leading.

For the Church of Smyrna, they had been oppressed and persecuted by the outside world for their faith. God tells them not to fear, for He will empower them to persevere. We need to possess this same level of confidence in God's promises to support us during our moments of opposition and difficulty. If we are fearful, then we will not be able to muster the endurance and perseverance we need to keep going. We need to be aware that since we are in opposition to this world, we will face persecution. Paul states in 2 Timothy 3:12, *"In fact, everyone who wants to live a godly life in Christ Jesus will be persecuted"*. Persecution can come in many forms: from resistance to removal, and even death. Because we know this is a fact, we need to resolve that we will stand firm, no matter what the persecution is. We will cling to Jesus and hold onto our faith.

Each individual and each church has a line of fear that they cannot seem to cross. This is a tactic by the enemy to delay what God is trying to do through us. We need to be willing to break down any obstacle that tries to set itself up against the Will of God. Relying on the promises of God's Word builds our faith and breaks down our fear. We need to have daily access to God's Word in multiple forms: through direct reading of scripture, praying the Word, listening to and gathering with other believers who reinforce the Word.

These opportunities will help us immerse ourselves in God's Word so that it will be all we depend on.

James 1:12 tells us, *"Blessed is the one who perseveres under trial because, having stood the test, that person will receive the crown of life that the Lord has promised to those who love him."* So, we know from this- there will be a test but if we persevere, we will receive the reward that God has promised. Now, this specifically mentions the crown of life, which is eternal life with God. However, perseverance will also produce a reward in the here and now as we will see the fruits of our labor for having stood the test. God will bless us for being obedient to His Will and standing firm in our faith when tested with trials. This does not mean things will be easy. It just means it will be possible, because with God, all things are possible.

Related to the concept of love from the previous chapter, Jesus tells us in Matthew 24 that in the later days, *"Because of the increase of wickedness, the love of most will grow cold, [13] but the one who stands firm (endures, perseveres) to the end will be saved."* We are being urged not to give-in or give-up even when what we see around us is dark and cold. These are the opportunities for our light to shine even brighter for Christ so that we create the true contrast with the world, just as Jesus did when He walked this earth. Do not let the trials of life dim you. Use this as kindling to spark the flames within you fueled by the power of the Holy Spirit.

Perseverance is not only important for what we will be able to do for others through it, but it also changes things within us and for us. There are many scriptures that speak of the benefits of perseverance. Most importantly is Romans 5:3-5, *"Not only so, but we also glory in our sufferings, because we know that suffering produces perseverance; 4 perseverance, character; and character, hope. 5 And hope does not put us to shame, because God's love has been poured out into our hearts through the Holy Spirit, who has been given to us."* These verses are clear: perseverance through trials is working for our good. We develop our character in a more Christ-like way and we renew our hope for what God will do.

As we learn to depend on Him in difficult circumstances, others are watching how we respond and seeing God at work in us. This speaks volumes in terms of a testimony and produces an authenticity that will draw others to you. We won't need to say much about our faith, because people will see what we believe and what we stand for by the way we respond to the circumstances in life.

In closing, the ultimate tool for our ability to stand and persevere is the Armor of God. Ephesians 6:13 says, *"Therefore put on the full armor of God, so that when the day of evil comes, you may be able to stand your ground, and after you have done everything, to stand."* The key here is not to withdraw and say, 'well God is going to handle it', but rather it is to do all we can according to the Word and leading of the Holy Spirit, and trust that God will do the rest. For too long, Christians have taken a back seat in fear of persecution or ridicule. We gain nothing from this, and in fact, we have lost a lot of ground from this mindset. God did not create us to be fearful of the world. He has given us the tools to stand-up against the world.

Ephesians goes on in verses 14-17 to tell us *"14 Stand firm then, with the belt of truth buckled around your waist, with the breastplate of righteousness in place, 15 and with your feet fitted with the readiness that comes from the gospel of peace. 16 In addition to all this, take up the shield of faith, with which you can extinguish all the flaming arrows of the evil one. 17 Take the helmet of salvation and the sword of the Spirit, which is the word of God."* God has more than amply prepared us for the battle. It is for us to be sure that we prepare ourselves each day. Therefore, be encouraged, do not fear and stand firm in the faith!

Integrity

The righteous man walks in his integrity; His children are blessed after him.

Proverbs 20:7

Integrity is characterized as having moral principles, uprightness, and honesty. These are characteristics that are severely lacking in the times we live in. This is because the world has become amoral. There is a general sense within society to do whatever is right for oneself with no reference or reverence for the law of God. Therefore, those who display the characteristics of integrity represent a stark contrast to the rest of the world.

The Church of Pergamos was given a reprimand that they had become too much like the world. There were those who were keeping the faith, while many had allowed their faith to be compromised by allowing pagan influence into the church. They were taken captive by false doctrine and allowed it to change them and what they believed. This was a compromise to their moral and spiritual integrity.

As believers, we are called to be set apart from the world and integrity is a key principle in living this out. Integrity can basically be broken down into three facets: integrity of thought, speech and action. All three of these facets have an influence on each other. How we think affects what we say and what we say affects how we act, and so on. True integrity in these facets will be evidence that we are following the Word of God. Our responses in each of these facets let others know who we are accountable to.

Integrity of thought can be guided by what Paul tells us in Romans 12:2, *"Do not conform to the pattern of this world, but be transformed by the renewing of your mind"*. We renew our mind by continually seeking the Word of God, so we do not fall prey to the enemy's schemes. Satan is the king of compromise. He will bend and manipulate truth in any way possible as to deceive and water down the power of The Word. If we bend our principles, lose our integrity or compromise our values in order to be liked by the world, then we are letting Satan win. This will undermine the authority of Christ and the Word of God, leaving us and our faith in a very vulnerable position. We need to guard our minds so that the truth of God's Word is our default setting.

Integrity of speech and action can be guided by Paul's advice in Colossians 4:5-6, *"Be wise in the way you act toward outsiders; make the most of every opportunity. 6 Let your conversation be always full of grace, seasoned with salt, so that you may know how to answer everyone."* While we speak and act in love, here again we should not compromise. Salt will be noticed and will get a reaction. Integrity in God's Word in how we speak and act will definitely make others pay attention. It is then when we will find an opportunity to engage with them.

Having integrity is important in the big and small things. It is how we should conduct our intimate affairs as well as our worldly responsibilities. People are watching us and how we respond. This matters because integrity has an impact on relationships as it leads to trust. When others recognize us as integris, they will want to be around us. They will engage with us and they will often ask us for our advice or opinion. This is the position we need to be in if we want to have influence.

Our goal is to have influence over others for the Kingdom. We should limit the influence that the world has on us. This is how we demonstrate integrity. James 4:4 tells us that any friend of the world is an enemy of God. While we absolutely have to function in the world, we should not carry ourselves as someone of the world (John 17:14-19). The world is going to pull us in so many ways, we cannot fall into the trap of being like it. We need to maintain our integrity so that we are displaying Jesus to everyone we encounter, and they are seeing that there are other options beyond what this world has to offer.

As with all of the characteristics we are exploring in this book, there is no expectation for perfection. However, a consistent effort to apply them and make better choices each day is the goal. Integrity depends on consistency. Consistency in our integrity is two-fold. First, we need to be mindful that we can't sometimes act with integrity and then other times not. We need to set our sights on being consistently integris in all of our interactions. Second, we need consistency between what we say and how we act. We cannot be saying one thing and then act in a completely different way. These slips in integrity will break the bonds of trust and cause us to lose the influence we have gained.

Integrity is a choice and there is a cost associated with it. We have to choose in each decision to continue to go back to biblical principles for how we speak and how we respond in each situation. This is where the rubber meets the road. If we can grab hold of this, then we have become doers of the Word, rather than just hearers. This is clearly going to have an impact on our life, but it also impacts everyone around us.

It has become commonplace today to adapt the mindset of 'go along to get along'. This is extremely dangerous for a Christian and it has had a long-lasting impact on our faith journey for ourselves and the next generation. Due to a weakening in our integrity as the Church, we have allowed so many things to get by us, resulting in negative consequences. This has led to an overall compromise of biblical values within society and even a compromise of God's Word within the Church. If The Church does not confront sin and call it out, it will eventually conform to the sin, making it no different from the rest of the world, as did happen with The Church of Pergamos.

Practically speaking, we need to become aware of the dynamics of crowd psychology and behavior. There is scientific evidence that individuals are influenced by others when in large groups. Research shows that an individual can have an elevated emotional response, become mindless, show a lack of self-control or act irrationally. It is so easy to just get caught up with whatever a group believes. What is the largest group or crowd we know? The World Wide Web and social media. This is the platform of a global crowd. Our children are being influenced every day by information and opinions that lack integrity and truth. It may not seem harmful at first, but these platforms have so much influence over this generation and are shaping what they believe.

A perfect biblical example of how this influence works is when Jesus was being accused before Pilate. The Bible says, there were a multitude of people that rose up to bring Jesus to Pilate. Although Jesus did not do what He was accused of and Pilate himself found no fault in him, the crowd still cheered to crucify Jesus. Barrabas was offered as a substitute, since he had clearly done what he was accused of. Yet the crowd set him free and shouted louder to crucify Jesus. Each time I reread this account in scripture, I have a physical and emotional response to it. First, there is a gnawing in my stomach imagining the people so evil as to send an innocent man to death in such a brutal way, forgetting the fact that this was God's son on top of that. And I am deeply saddened to think how many times we have followed the crowd, knowing it went against the truth or compromised our principles?

Because of social media, this generation is experiencing this phenomena for the first time in history on such a large scale. The youth of today are bombarded daily with so much pressure from the world on all fronts. There is a 24/7 stream of influence to sway them to believe one way or another. While not all of social media is bad, the enemy has used it to influence their minds, their bodies and their very souls. There has been so much damage caused by access to these platforms. This has been a major tool in the hijacking of a generation. So many of the youth are literally (in some cases) dying to follow it and be accepted by it.

The mob mentality can be so dangerous and we are now seeing the true manifestation of its consequences. We need to guard the children in what they are being exposed to and teach them that they do not have to fall in line with what social media says. This can be done by setting a firm foundation in our homes based on what The Word of God says. Let's make a habit of allowing our children to see us go to the Bible for an answer to something rather than going to Google. This type of foundation will help them respond to the world with integrity rather than cave into peer pressure.

It is clear that social media is not going anywhere, so we need parameters for how to safely manage it for ourselves and our family. We need to try and untangle ourselves from the grip of this web. We also need mindfulness for how we present ourselves on these platforms. Are we being integris and engaging in a manner that will glorify God?

It takes courage to make hard choices. There are so few people who will actually stand for their principles when they might differ from the crowd. This is our test. Sometimes God puts us in difficult circumstances so we have to make a choice. This will test our integrity and character. If everything was easy, then it would not be a choice but a default setting. Let's agree to not settle for safe or easy- let's be bold for The Kingdom. The next generation of believers are counting on us.

We are told in scripture that the world will hate us because we follow Christ. We need to enter into every situation aware of the fact that we are different. We will most likely encounter opposition because we are counter to culture. This will definitely rub some people the wrong way because they are following the spirit of the world, not the Holy Spirit. The difference will be in how we respond. We need to take a stand, speak the truth in love and refuse to compromise our principles, doing so with confidence knowing that God will protect us in the midst of it all.

Warnings and Encouragement from

the Book of Luke

Meanwhile, when a crowd of many thousands had gathered, so that they were trampling on one another, Jesus began to speak first to his disciples, saying: "Be on your guard against the yeast of the Pharisees, which is hypocrisy. 2 There is nothing concealed that will not be disclosed, or hidden that will not be made known. 3 What you have said in the dark will be heard in the daylight, and what you have whispered in the ear in the inner rooms will be proclaimed from the roofs.

4 "I tell you, my friends, do not be afraid of those who kill the body and after that can do no more. 5 But I will show you whom you should fear: Fear him who, after your body has been killed, has authority to throw you into hell. Yes, I tell you, fear him. 6 Are not five sparrows sold for two pennies? Yet not one of them is forgotten by God. 7 Indeed, the very hairs of your head are all numbered. Don't be afraid; you are worth more than many sparrows.

8 *"I tell you, whoever publicly acknowledges me before others, the Son of Man will also acknowledge before the angels of God. 9 But whoever disowns me before others will be disowned before the angels of God. 10 And everyone who speaks a word against the Son of Man will be forgiven, but anyone who blasphemes against the Holy Spirit will not be forgiven.*

11 *"When you are brought before synagogues, rulers and authorities, do not worry about how you will defend yourselves or what you will say, 12 for the Holy Spirit will teach you at that time what you should say."*

Luke 12: 1-12

Discernment

The person without the Spirit does not accept the things that come from the Spirit of God but considers them foolishness, and cannot understand them because they are discerned only through the Spirit. 15 The person with the Spirit makes judgments about all things, but such a person is not subject to merely human judgments, 16 for, "Who has known the mind of the Lord so as to instruct him?" But we have the mind of Christ.

1 Corinthians 2:14-16

Charles Spurgeon, a well-known theologian said, "discernment is not knowing the difference between right and wrong, but rather knowing the difference between right and almost right." It is critical that we are aware of this distinction. Discernment is accountable to truth. In this time and season, our level of discernment needs to be extremely high. The enemy has increased his wickedness and deception, so that even the elect might be deceived (Matthew 24:24).

1 Corinthians 2:15 says we are to apply this discernment in all things, which means we need to be discerning in personal matters, family matters, societal matters, but most importantly spiritual matters. If we say we are believers and unite with other believers, then discernment should be of utmost importance in spiritual matters. We need to be clear about what we believe.

Discernment comes from the Spirit and The Word. This world is complex and we are complex. Since we are created in the image of God, like the Trinity, He created us having three dimensions: a soul (our mind, feelings, etc), a body and a spirit. One distinction between humans and other animals is that God made other animals having just the soul and a body. He exclusively decided to give us as humans a spirit so we could be connected to Him. This is profound. Not only was this for the purpose of creating the relationship He desired with us, but because He is expecting us to act differently than other animals who respond with fleshly instincts.

Therefore, if we make decisions or respond only according to the flesh, we are missing-out on the divine guidance that flows directly from God to help us make good decisions.

Discernment is also developed from an intimate knowledge of God's Word. When we know the Word of God deeply, we think differently. We cannot discern the Will of God if we do not know the Word of God. We encounter massive amounts of information daily as we navigate life and make decisions. Sifting through it all and making good choices is dependent on discernment. Not filtering what the world gives us through the lens of scripture can set us up for all kinds of hurt. Sometimes we can recover from bad choices quickly and other times it may be more difficult. The latter are the ones that tend to have an impact on others as well. God has given us access to His Word and His Spirit, so we can avoid some of this strife.

We mentioned earlier in a previous chapter Paul's advice from Romans 12:2, *"Do not conform to the pattern of this world, but be transformed by the renewing of your mind."* However, it goes on to say, *"then you will be able to test and approve what God's will is—his good, pleasing and perfect will."* Here again, biblical literacy is key. This will help guide us in knowing who and what we are dealing with in this world. No matter what the situation is, it has to be held up to the Word of God. Then we will be able to rightly discern truth from error.

The Church of Thyatira in Revelation fell prey to false prophets and doctrines because they lacked discernment. They let their guard down and because of this lack of discernment, idolatry and immorality entered into their church. We are once more seeing this again in the churches of today. It has fallen into all types of immorality and false doctrines.

Those of us with discernment cannot simply sit by and be okay when false doctrine and immorality are being accepted and even celebrated within the Church. We need to take a stand and guard against this. We should not be complacent while this is happening on our watch. We will be accountable to this in our day of judgment, but in the here and now it has tremendous implications for the next generation of faith.

The lack of discernment within The Church is leaving young, impressionable believers confused. Imagine it from their perspective: "Why is it okay to be homosexual in the church down the street, but it is not okay here?" This leads a person to believe that this is an opinion or matter of choice, rather than a matter that has biblical reference which determines it to be a sin. That person will most likely choose to then go to the place where they are accepted rather than stay where they are asked to reflect upon or repent for their choices. Once that happens, we then lose access to guide and mentor that person according to truth and love and then they are lost.

Make no mistake, discernment will cause division. It will separate those who truly follow the Word and Spirit and those who don't. We cannot make this a reason why we don't apply discernment to the best of our ability. Corinthians 2:14-16 tells us that because we have the Holy Spirit, we will be considered foolish by the rest of the world. Christians as a whole already have a certain reputation. Therefore, engaging with non-believers and those who are seeking needs to be done in a discerning manner. We need to take the lead of the Holy Spirit to show us who, where, when and how to engage effectively.

In order to be able to apply discernment appropriately, we need to remember the advice from the previous chapter about love, always keeping in mind being compassionate to others without compromising the moral integrity of God's Word. Today's generation is so easily offended by many things. This is because society has defined differences of opinion or correction as hateful. We need to approach others with understanding, even if we are not in agreement. Correction without judgment is necessary. Being discerning is not about being judgmental in the manner which the world perceives it. Rather, it is setting things straight according to the truth of God's Word.

Wisdom and discernment go hand-in-hand. Ephesians 5:15-17 tells us, *"Be very careful, then, how you live—not as unwise but as wise, 16 making the most of every opportunity, because the days are evil. 17 Therefore do not be foolish, but understand what the Lord's will is."* We need to care about truth and take God's Word seriously. It should be the guide to all things. The Bible also tells us if we do not have wisdom, we can ask for it and God will give it generously (James 1:5). Therefore, there is no reason for us to wrestle with the ways of the world when we have God's wisdom.

When we choose to not depend on God's wisdom or not conduct ourselves in a discerning way, it can cost us dearly. It will allow us to make choices that are not in our best interests, the Church's best interest or the nation's best interest. We have recently witnessed this in world events during the Covid Pandemic. We saw how a lack of discernment on a large scale led to chaos, loss of freedom and even death. People were entrenched in what the world was saying without using discernment and did many irrational things. Those who fared best during this time were those who leaned in and clung to the wisdom of God.

God has equipped us with a sound mind to be able to rightfully divide everything that we encounter. The best way I have found to build discernment is through regular scripture reading and prayer. Reading and studying God's Word daily helps us to internalize it. It becomes part of who we are and how we think. We are told in 1 Peter 3:15 to always be ready with a response when others ask us about the Lord. It is so much quicker and easier to be discerning when we know what scripture says. Knowing God's Word on a deep level also allows us to hear God's voice and know it is from Him. It will resonate with our spirit and make it clear how we should respond.

In addition, prayer is one of the most powerful tools we have, and it is often underutilized. Prayer is direct communication with God, through His spirit and ours. This heightens our awareness of God, which increases our discernment. Prayer helps bring wisdom and clarity to a situation so we can begin to see from God's perspective. This is so important as we go out into the world and engage with those who do not believe. We always want to be moving according to

God's guidance. Prayer will communicate to us, where He wants us to go, who He wants us to impact and what He wants us to say.

Because there has been a significant gap within The Church on possessing and applying the skills of daily scripture reading and prayer, so many in this generation do not know the truth. This opens them up to become an easy target for the enemy. We need to build up biblical literacy within The Church so those who are attending services or church events will have a solid foundation in The Word.

It is quite unbelievable that so many churches never open the Bible. Imagine if your child was going to medical school to be a surgeon and was never asked once by any of his or her professors to open an anatomy book. Would you consider them to be adequately trained for the job? We must adequately train the next generation to hold the line of faith. There is a common saying, 'If you don't know what you stand for, you will fall for anything.' Many of the youth are not equipped to handle what the world is throwing at them because they do not have a foundation in truth. Biblical literacy is a cornerstone of the faith. We cannot rightfully defend something we don't know or understand. If we are knowledgeable about God's Word, then we can be confident. And when we are confident, we can stand.

Authenticity

*As a prisoner for the Lord, then, I urge you to live a
life worthy of the calling you have received.*

Ephesians 4:1

We are told to live a life worthy of being
called a follower of Christ (Ephesians 4:1). The
characteristics that follow in chapter 4 of Ephesians
outlines humility, patience and love as part of what
it means to be worthy. These are also the
characteristics of authenticity and spiritual maturity.
Living in this manner brings unity to the body of
Christ.

So much of what we encounter today is
fake. We are living in a time that can be
characterized as 'virtual' reality. So many things we
interact with and depend on daily are virtual or
artificial. As the name suggests, these things are
not real, but almost seem real. Many of these
things may even be accompanied by going through

the motions as if certain things are real, yet that doesn't change the fact that these things still do not exist authentically. This has given us a deceptive and false sense of fullness. We believe that we have everything, but in actuality, none of what we 'have' is real.

Many have grown accustomed to virtual communication, virtual currency, virtual pets and even virtual mates. We consume artificial food, admire artificial flowers, and may soon be replaced by artificial intelligence. This is not to say that true fulfillment should come from earthly or material things, but as humans, we recognize that we do have basic earthly needs that help us to be healthy and balanced individuals, and therefore need to connect to society as it is.

In actuality, a huge void and sense of emptiness has been created for many in this virtual movement. So many people lack engagement, true communication and real relationships in this virtual space. As a result, when one encounters authenticity, it is rather refreshing. Because this gap has been created between the authentic and the virtual, it has opened an opportunity like never before to build real and genuine relationships with others who may have been marginalized by the virtual movement. It is fertile ground to reach out with the authentic love of Christ. Our first step is to really reach out in our community and see where there is need. Building networks to support people authentically in these needs is essential. We need to meet people's basic natural needs as well as their spiritual needs.

My goal is never to lead someone to a particular denomination or organization, so this reference is purely for context only. The Salvation Army has been in existence since 1865. I cannot speak to all of their dealings, but they are a presence in the community and have had an impact since their inception. Why I mention them here is because the founders William and Catherine Booth had the right intention on how to authentically reach people for the Kingdom. They started the organization with the principle of soup, soap and salvation. They believed that once you could meet the basic needs of an individual, then you can authentically share The Gospel.

This touches on the idea of knowing and understanding who we will be ministering to. We need to care enough to get to know those who are lost or seeking in a genuine way. When we know the person, then we can develop the plan for how to authentically reach them.

Building a relationship will be helpful. We are told in scripture that fellowship amongst believers is important. We should not deny gathering to pray, commune and encourage one another. We should consider how we widen this circle to bring others in. Never underestimate the power of an invite and a bit of persistence. We can ask someone to be included ten times, but they only need to say yes once. Inviting others to see faith in action can be very powerful when it is authentic. We don't want to be a fellowship of believers who are just going through the motions. We want to walk, talk and be authentic in our faith.

If we are living authentically for Christ, then we should also be speaking authentically. Scripture has a lot to say about our words and the impact they have. We know how influential words can be for either building things up or tearing things down. In Matthew 12:36, Jesus tells us that we will be held accountable for every idle word on judgment day. Others will hold us to our word as well, so we should be sure that it is genuine and authentic. How we speak to others will show our sincerity in following Christ.

The church of Sardis in Revelation is warned about their lack of authenticity in their faith. They are going through the motions but are told that they are spiritually dead. This is because they were not relying on the Holy Spirit. The Holy Spirit brings us authenticity as believers. It is because He works through us that others may believe. This is what it means to be in the fullness of Christ.

Many churches today lack this same awareness of and reliance upon The Holy Spirit in their general functionality. When we are guided by The Spirit, we move in power. This will make us more effective and will make others take notice. If we want to be powerful Christians and have impact, we need the Holy Spirit's guidance.

Understanding who He is and how He works in us is essential. This is what sets us apart from this world.

We discussed in chapter one about being purposeful, intentional and explicit about our faith. Intentionality and authenticity go hand-in-hand because they relate back to our identity. Who do we identify as or with? Do we truly believe our identity is in Christ? We will either belong to the world or belong to Christ. We cannot be authentic to others if we are not authentic to ourselves first. Do we walk as if our identity is in Christ? We are set apart because we have the Holy Spirit within us. This makes a difference in us. The Holy Spirit has to be our center and guide so we can live authentically and share that authenticity with others. If we are walking authentically in the fullness of Christ, then we won't easily be taken captive by the things of the world.

Colossians 2:8-10 warns us to be aware that we are not taken captive by hollow or deceptive philosophies. There is so much in this world trying to distract us. This is really aimed at taking away our identity in Christ. The ultimate example of this starts at the very beginning. As we know, God is the original Creator. He created us uniquely and authentically. Satan from the start has wanted to be like God but cannot. He is also unable to create anything original or authentic. Therefore, Satan must twist, manipulate and distort things to get what he wants. Something that is in opposition to the original is a counterfeit. Until Christ's return, Satan is the ruler over this world. Therefore, we should not be surprised by many counterfeits and false prophets. Many aspects of our daily life have been tainted by this manipulation. Do not be deceived.

Science is this world's god. We are quite aware that science has been trying to copy what God has done since its existence. They have made some advancements, but nothing is comparable to the original work of God. We now see through technology their desire to create like God has grown even more fervent. They have the capability to make and alter body parts, and even entire living things. They have even created artificial wombs to grow embryos in, to try to recreate human life.

We also know that artificial Intelligence has taken a stronghold in society and will move with lightning speed forward. The long-term effects of these advancements will not be positive because they are counterfeits and did not come from God, but the world.

We mentioned social media in the previous chapter and spoke of the dangers it holds. It too hosts massive amounts of counterfeits. These platforms twist and distort information and stories to make it appear as truth. This is done with the intention to deceive and manipulate those who consume it. We are literally in a time when we cannot believe our own eyes. So many things we encounter can be counterfeit of some kind. For one thing, this should put us on alert, and as we discussed in the previous chapter, we should heighten our discernment. But more importantly this is an opportunity to share truth and be authentic, letting others know that real truth comes from God's Word, and that Jesus is truth!

It is only natural that this acceptance of virtual, artificial and counterfeit everything has made its way into the Church as well. So much so, that there is even a counterfeit version of Jesus. This is a version of 'Jesus' that looks like this world, one who loves without the need for repentance. A 'Jesus' that is flashy but fake. Of all the aforementioned counterfeits, this is by far the most dangerous for the faith and for the souls of those who encounter it. There is no salvation from this counterfeit 'Jesus' and yet so many are eagerly following this version of 'Jesus' that is not biblical.

Progressive Christianity is one such modern-day movement that totally stripped away all of the authenticity of being Christian. It believes that Jesus was a good person and a smart teacher. It speaks of love being important, but there is no repentance, no salvation and not adhering to the infallible word of scripture. In fact, this is a Marxist religion under the guise of 'Christianity'. One may not realize that they are following this type of movement because it so cleverly blends in with the thinking of the world. You may not be attending a progressive church, but be on the lookout for progressive views that are creeping in. Be alert, sober minded and don't be afraid to authentically speak out if there is something not biblical in your church.

Taking advice from Paul in 2 Timothy 2:15, he tells us to, *"Do your best to present yourself to God as one approved, a worker who does not need to be ashamed and who correctly handles the word of truth."* In order to represent the true, authentic and one and only biblical Jesus to others, we cannot compromise the Word of God even an inch. If we do, it creates a slippery slope leading to destructive division and splintered doctrine. Instead of giving others a watered-down version of The Gospel, let's introduce them to the living water of the genuine Jesus Christ.

Instructions for Christian Living

17 So I tell you this, and insist on it in the Lord, that you must no longer live as the Gentiles do, in the futility of their thinking. 18 They are darkened in their understanding and separated from the life of God because of the ignorance that is in them due to the hardening of their hearts. 19 Having lost all sensitivity, they have given themselves over to sensuality so as to indulge in every kind of impurity, and they are full of greed. 20 That, however, is not the way of life you learned 21 when you heard about Christ and were taught in him in accordance with the truth that is in Jesus. 22 You were taught, with regard to your former way of life, to put off your old self, which is being corrupted by its deceitful desires; 23 to be made new in the attitude of your minds; 24 and to put on the new self, created to be like God in true righteousness and holiness. 25 Therefore each of you must put off falsehood and speak truthfully to your neighbor, for we are all members of one body. 26 "In your anger do not sin": Do not let the sun go down while you are still angry, 27 and do not give the devil a *foothold. **28** Anyone who has been stealing must steal no longer, but must work, doing something useful with their own hands, that they may have something to share with those in need. **29** Do not let any unwholesome talk come out of your mouths, but only what is helpful for building others up according to their needs, that it may benefit those who listen. **30** And do not grieve the Holy Spirit of God, with whom you were sealed for the day of redemption. **31** Get rid of all bitterness, rage and anger, brawling and slander, along with every form of malice. **32** Be kind and compassionate to one another, forgiving each other, just as in Christ God forgave you.*

Ephesians 4:17-32

Strength

And pray that we may be delivered from wicked and evil people, for not everyone has faith. 3 But the Lord is faithful, and he will strengthen you and protect you from the evil one.

2 Thessalonians 3:3

The Church of Philadelphia was not given any reprimand, but God acknowledged that they were weak. This church faced a lot of hostility from the outside world and it was met with trials of all kinds, so this made them weak. God reassured them that He would provide them with the strength they needed.

These words are so comforting even to us, because we too might feel weak and battle-worn from the cares and concerns of this world. But take heart; God promises to give us strength in trials and tribulations. No one is exempt from struggle on this earth. In 2 Thessalonians 3:3, it tells us that the faithfulness of God is what gives us strength.

It is important to understand that strength does not come from us, but from God. It is because of what God did and does that we can have hope, confidence, and strength to move forward. We are not doing life alone if we let God lead us and strengthen us.

The testimony of what God has done in us and through us in some of our most difficult circumstances gives hope to others. When they see what God has brought us through, they start to think differently about their own situation. This is the evidence of God's faithfulness, 1 Peter 4:11 says, *"If anyone speaks, they should do so as one who speaks the very words of God. If anyone serves, they should do so with the strength God provides, so that in all things God may be praised through Jesus Christ. To him be the glory and the power for ever and ever."* God will faithfully help us in our time of struggle and need, but we must give glory to God for it.

There is no surprise that in our society that is so focused on self, there is a trend of falling into a victim mindset. Once things don't go our way or we have been hurt by someone else, we resort to thinking that we are owed something in return to repair or restore the damage that was caused. In this type of thinking, others are blamed for our actions rather than taking responsibility for things ourselves. This is a completely flesh-driven response and lacks any spiritual discernment. The enemy uses this tactic to weaken us. If we are always the victim, then we cannot be the victor!

We want to be in a position of strength as believers, not weakened by the lies of the enemy. We need to break the stronghold of the victim mindset and rely on God's strength to get us over the hurts of life. Let's not stay stuck in a bad place. Allowing the Holy Spirit to guide us out of the dark places will help us shine brightly for The Kingdom.

Most people relate to strength in a physical sense. That does play a role in Kingdom work, but more often than not, it requires strength of a different kind. The enemy has one goal: to stop us from doing the work of God. He will use any tactic necessary to do so. Exerting pressure in our lives from all sides is a common mechanism he uses.

If he cannot turn us from God, he will try to weaken us. Resisting these pressures takes strength and fortitude of a spiritual kind.

Paul speaks of this in 2 Corinthians 12:8-10, *"Three times I pleaded with the Lord to take it away from me. 9 But he said to me, "My grace is sufficient for you, for my power is made perfect in weakness." Therefore I will boast all the more gladly about my weaknesses, so that Christ's power may rest on me. 10 That is why, for Christ's sake, I delight in weaknesses, in insults, in hardships, in persecutions, in difficulties. For when I am weak, then I am strong."* Paul was clearly in a deep struggle. Most theologians agree that this was not of a physical nature. Paul was wrestling with something internal and probably demonic. However, he rested in the fact that God's grace and strength would see him through.

In addition, from these verses, Paul gives us a lesson about submitting. He recognized that he had to give it over to God. Interestingly, Paul first tried to pray and plead with God to change the situation. However, when God did not answer as he had hoped, Paul let it all go into the hands of God for His grace, mercy and strength to sustain him. You see, we are partly weak because we try to control the circumstances around us. We are trying to keep it all together on our own. If we are trying to do things in our own strength, we will tire easily and become less effective.

Depending on God's grace and strength will allow us to do miraculous things. This is our testimony. It will confound the world and cause people to inquire about how we managed it. It will be evident that it could not have been accomplished by human means, which will present the opportunity to point the glory to God for the victory.

The words of Isaiah beautifully and poetically describe what it is like to depend on God for strength. It says in Isaiah 40:29 -31, *"He gives strength to the weary and increases the power of the weak. 30 Even youths grow tired and weary, and young men stumble and fall; 31 but those who hope in the LORD, will renew their strength. They will soar on wings like eagles; they will run and not grow weary, they will walk and not be faint."*

It doesn't say in these verses that we won't grow tired or weary, but it says that we will be renewed in our strength because we put our hope and trust in God and what He can do. He is the one who will lift us up and keep us going. We are not in this alone.

Another type of strength comes when taking a stand. This is a powerful statement and can be a unifying action. There is a blessing that comes along with standing strong for our faith. We will realize this, not only in our own lives, but in the ability that we will have to pass that faith to the next generation because we took that stand.

This type of stand for faith will clearly have us relying again on the advice of Ephesians 6 for putting on the full armor of God. Verses 10 -11 tell us, *"Finally, be strong in the Lord and in his mighty power. 11 Put on the full armor of God, so that you can take your stand against the devil's schemes."*

Here again we are reminded that strength is not from us, but from the Lord.

Just as we exercise to build our physical strength, we also need to exercise our mind and spirit to build our spiritual strength. We do this through daily prayer and scripture reading, but we also practice each time we are tested. Exercise is meant to help us build resistance to pressure and stressors that may come against the body. Spiritual exercise is just what we need to build ourselves up against the stressors of this world. We need to stay sharp so that we can properly respond to and address the needs of The Church. Our collective strength in the faith is magnified by the strength of each individual believer.

It will be difficult for one person to stand for faith, but when many believers stand firm, we are effective in holding the line. This will leave us with the legacy of faith to pass down to the next generation. God promises that there will always be a remnant of believers who will remain, but let us be the generation that delivers Him a Kingdom of believers, by His might and for His glory!

Commitment

And whatever you do, whether in word or deed, do it all in the name of the Lord Jesus, giving thanks to God the Father through him.

Colossians 3:17

God is not looking for fence-sitters. He is seeking those who are serious and committed. Trying to have one foot in the world and the other in the Kingdom does not work, for ourselves or for the next generation of believers. How can we get others excited to follow Jesus and build their faith, if we ourselves are lukewarm? This generation wants to be committed and passionate about something, yet they look for it in many of the wrong places. This is why there is so much rebellion, protests and atypical behaviors in mass. They are crying out to put their passion into something meaningful. The world has accepted this and channeled it into so many ungodly movements.

Are we actively trying to capture the passion of the youth just as rigorously?

When we reflect our commitment and passion for Christ in meaningful and powerful ways, it is contagious. Others want what we have. This does not mean that we need to be evangelizing on the street corner. Colossians 3:17 says that whatever we do, do it for the Lord. That is commitment! So if you are a stay at home mom, that is your mission field. Teach your children The Word and help them develop good biblical habits. If you work in an office, show and share your commitment to Christ with your colleagues. This does not have to be in word but in deed. Go the extra mile and always present yourself worthily.

If you are an educator, treat your students and parents with respect even if it is not reciprocated. Pray for those students who are hurting. Make your classroom a place that is ran on biblical principles, even if you cannot speak them out directly.

The Church of Laodicea was given the harshest warning by God because they were lukewarm. God said that He would spit them out of His mouth. This is like washing His hands with them. He would not want anything to do with them. That is a scary thought, to have God be so upset that He just turns away from us. Laodicea lacked commitment as they professed that they believed, but they became complacent. Things were going well for them and seeking God was just not so important anymore.

Commitment over complacency as instructed to the Church of Laodicea is what is needed in our time as well. When we were in a time of such prosperity as a nation, and for most, at an individual level, we took our sights off the fact that this prosperity came from the Hand of God. We forgot to be thankful, we forgot to acknowledge Him, and we forgot to give Him the glory for it. Now that the world around us is slipping into decline, we as a Church are realizing that we let go of our commitment to God and have become lukewarm about the importance of spiritual matters.

So how do we get back on track? Looking again at Colossians 3:17 for guidance, it says do all things in the name of the Lord. This sets up an understanding that this is a way of living, a lifestyle, not just something we say we believe. Others need to see that we have made a full commitment to Christ and we do not waiver from it. That requires us to examine all things that we partake in and reflect on if these things honor God.

There are several things that we need to consider when we take this inventory and there is scripture to guide each one. The first thing we need to consider is who we associate with. While we are not told to completely disengage from the rest of the world, we are told to be mindful of who we are in close relationships with. 1 Corinthians 15:33 tells us, *"Do not be misled: "Bad company corrupts good character."* It is hard to stay committed to Christ if we are constantly influenced by non-believers.

We also need to be mindful of what takes up our time and 'entertains' us. This can be the types of movies and music we consume or the activities that we support. Satan uses these tools as gateways into ungodly thinking. So many people think that this is harmless fun, but Satan doesn't see it that way. He sees it as an opportunity to separate us from our commitment to God.

Another area to examine in this respect is our church affiliation. We need to be sure that we are being influenced in a biblically sound way and guided by the Holy Spirit by those who are leading us. As we discussed in a previous chapter, the church has a specific role. They are not to control you, but to guide you and help you be accountable to your commitment to God.

Commitment is kept through reinforcement. We should daily affirm that we are committed to Christ no matter what comes our way. We should agree each day when we wake up that we will live for the Lord. Verbally making this commitment each day already puts the enemy on notice that you will not be taken advantage of easily.

We need to be on guard because our commitment can be shaken by doubt.

Doubt actually shows a lack of commitment. It can be subtle and we may not recognize it. Doubt robs us of so many blessings from God because we are scared to commit and move forward into what God is calling us to do.

This is even true in close intimate matters with God Himself, such as prayer. James 1:6-8 puts it this way; *"But when you ask, you must believe and not doubt, because the one who doubts is like a wave of the sea, blown and tossed by the wind. 7 That person should not expect to receive anything from the Lord. 8 Such a person is double-minded and unstable in all they do."* If we say we are committed to God, then we need to be all-in without wavering.

We can overcome doubt by firmly taking a stand and having others keep us accountable for it, just like Joshua did when he stood before all the tribes of Israel in Joshua 24:15 and said, *"As for me and my house we will serve the Lord."* He asked the others to be witnesses to it and commit to it as well. The people stood with Joshua and agreed. Joshua then told them to remove the old idols and to turn their hearts to the Lord from that day forward. This commitment was recorded in stone, not just as a reminder, but as a tool for accountability. If they were to break their commitment, the stones would be witness against them (Joshua 24).

We need reminders in our life to keep us accountable, focused and committed. This can be accomplished in many ways and we should do as The Spirit leads. Most importantly, this can be done by surrounding ourselves with other believers. They will reinforce biblical principles in action and help us stay on track. Daily reading of scripture, prayer and journaling can help us stay grounded in our commitment. You may also consider a banner, or scripture displayed prominently in your home that catches your attention and can encourage you each day to stay on track. We pray that you will take a stand today, for yourself, your family and your home to be committed to serving the Lord!

"If you love Christ, never be ashamed to let others see it and know it. Speak for Him. Witness for Him. Live for Him." ~ J.C. Ryle

www.rylequotes.org

Paul's Final Warning to the Church of Corinth

Examine yourselves to see whether you are in the faith; test yourselves. Do you not realize that Christ Jesus is in you—unless, of course, you fail the test? 6 And I trust that you will discover that we have not failed the test. 7 Now we pray to God that you will not do anything wrong—not so that people will see that we have stood the test but so that you will do what is right even though we may seem to have failed. 8 For we cannot do anything against the truth, but only for the truth.

2 Corinthians 13: 5-8

Conclusion

I enjoy writing books, not that it is easy. A lot of study, research and prayer goes into the content that is developed to fill the pages. However, in the process I always feel that I have learned even more than I may have contributed. I value this time and process because God fills it with so many lessons. After all, nothing worthwhile comes easy. Our faith is a worthwhile cause to dedicate time, study and mediation to. Then we can present ourselves as approved before the Lord. However, this is just building head knowledge. The required next step is the application of what was learned so we can walk worthy of our calling.

If we want the next generation to pick up the faith, then we have to pass it on. As is true for most characteristics and behaviors to be learned, we need to set an example and be a role model for how they are applied. Are we loving our neighbor or talking gossip behind their back? Are we taking a stand or sitting on the sidelines? Are we on our phones or in the Bible? We cannot ask others to do what we don't do ourselves.

Really grasping our role and responsibility as it relates to our faith and the passing down of it to future generations can certainly be overwhelming. Luke 12:48 reminds us that *"...From everyone who has been given much, much will be demanded; and from the one who has been entrusted with much, much more will be asked."* Consider what God has given to us through Christ. We have received freedom, salvation and eternal life. Who are we to keep this only for ourselves or to squander the blessings of God? It is our obligation to share with and encourage those who come after to grasp these same blessings that are being freely offered to them. The challenge is they need to understand that these are there for the asking. This is where we come in, making it known!

The encouraging part is that God never once said that we were in this alone. He has equipped us in so many ways to do this work. He has given us His Word and He has also given us His Spirit, which is enough.

But he did not stop there. He also gave us a community of believers, The Church body, to share in this work together. Let's agree to commit to this work and be accountable to one another to see it through.

I sincerely believe that the next generation is seeking and ready to hear the Good News, it just needs to be done in a way that they can access it. The darker the world becomes the brighter the light will shine. There are young hearts waiting to hear the truth. I pray that we do not miss out on any opportunity to make the truth known to them, always with our focus on Jesus, because He is the Way, the Truth and the Life. Someone's life may literally depend on it.

Remember, Rely, Reflect

Our goal for this book was to give you practical insights and tools to help make the most of every opportunity for sharing the faith. Using Christ as our model, we should always be focused on love and truth. Jesus is the embodiment of compassion without compromise. The three key actionable steps from this book that can help us do this, are summed up in the following: Remember, Rely, Reflect.

As we shared in the first chapter of this book, **remember** to be Purposeful, Intentional and Explicit (PIE) about your faith each day. Through our words and actions, we have the potential to make Christ known to so many. Wherever God has placed you, we encourage you to start small and start now. Reach out to those in your sphere of influence who are being deceived by this world.

It can never be overstated that we need to **rely** on the full Armor of God (Ephesians 6:10-17) daily. Without having the proper mindset, tools and guidance we will not be successful addressing the things we come against in this world. Go into the world in confidence because He has given you this armor. Prayer is also mentioned in Ephesians 6 directly after the armor. Prayer is so underestimated. We know how important communication is in our daily interactions and often we forget to communicate with the most important person, our Abba- Father.

Reflect upon the advice given to the Seven Churches of Revelation mentioned throughout the bulk of this book. This advice tells us to love deeply, have perseverance, show integrity, use discernment, display authenticity, depend on God's strength and fully commit to Christ in our own life. Which ones do we recognize in our own life? Which ones do we need to build-up? We will receive the rewards for keeping the faith. Therefore, let us embrace what God has set before us for advancing the Kingdom, having an impact and influence for the glory of God wherever He has called us. God Bless you on this journey.

Hear this, you elders; listen, all who live in the land.

Has anything like this ever happened in your days

or in the days of your ancestors?

Tell it to your children, and let your children tell it to their children,

and their children to the next generation.

Joel 1:2-3

References

1. "'Ecosexual' woman claims she's in love with oak tree." *New York Post*, 26 December 2023, https://nypost.com/2023/12/26/lifestyle/ecosexual-woman-claims-shes-in-love-with-oak-tree/. Accessed 28 April 2024.

2. "PIE Guide" https://www.languagemagazine.com/internetedition/langmag_pages/ProvidingDirect_LM07.pdf

3. "Love embraces and resists | Bethany." *Bethany Christian Services*, https://bethany.org/resources/love-embraces-and-resists. Accessed 27 April 2024.

4. Mcleod, Saul. "Maslow's Hierarchy of Needs." *Simply Psychology*, 24 January 2024, https://www.simplypsychology.org/maslow.html. Accessed 27 April 2024.

5. Munsil, Tracy F. "New Study Shows Shocking Lack of Biblical Worldview Among American Pastors." *Arizona Christian University*, 12 May 2022, https://www.arizonachristian.edu/2022/05/12/shocking-lack-of-biblical-worldview-among-american-pastors. Accessed 27 April 2024.

6. "The Narrow Path." *Facebook*, https://www.facebook.com/NarrowVsBroaderPath. Accessed 28 April 2024.

7. Pruitt, Shane. "Shane Pruitt on X: "4-generation fade: 1) parents don't make church a high priority for their kids 2) kids grow up & make it less of a priority for their kids 3) those kids grow up & make it no priority for their kids 4) those kids grow up w/ no concept of God." *X.com*, 9 June 2021, https://twitter.com/shane_pruitt78/status/1402707285785333761. Accessed 27 April 2024.

8. Ryle, JC. "J.C. Ryle Quotes." *J.C. Ryle Quotes*, https://www.rylequotes.org/quotes. Accessed 27 April 2024.
    Seaman, Andrew. "A New Chapter in Millennial Church Attendance." *Barna Group*, 4 August 2022, https://www.barna.com/research/church-attendance-2022/. Accessed 27 April 2024.

Milton Keynes UK
Ingram Content Group UK Ltd.
UKHW020704120624
443828UK00007B/50